I Found God Outside Of Church

Mary Louise

© 2021 Mary Louise. All rights reserved.

Scripture quotations marked (KJV) are taken from the King James version of the Bible.

Scripture quotations marked (NIV) are taken from the Holy Bible, New International Version®, NIV®. Copyright © 1973, 1978, 1984, 2011 by Biblica, Inc.™ Used by permission of Zondervan. All rights reserved worldwide. www.zondervan.com The "NIV" and "New International Version" are trademarks registered in the United States Patent and Trademark Office by Biblica, Inc.™

Scripture quotations marked (NKJV) are taken from the New King James Version®. Copyright © 1982 by Thomas Nelson. Used by permission. All rights reserved.

Scripture quotations marked (NLT) are taken from the Holy Bible, New Living Translation, copyright ©1996, 2004, 2015 by Tyndale House Foundation. Used by permission of Tyndale House Publishers, Inc., Carol Stream, Illinois 60188. All rights reserved.

Printed in the United States of America.

ISBN 978-1-7375710-0-1

I dedicate this book to all Jews –
God's chosen people.

Contents

1. Where I Found God — 7
2. Bad Church Experiences — 17
3. The Worst Thing and the Best Thing — 27
4. Passing Him By — 33
5. Tired — 41
6. Lost — 43
7. Running — 45
8. Brazil — 47
9. Adventure — 53
10. Other Church Experiences — 57
11. Timing — 65
12. Obstacle to Breakthrough — 69
13. Tools for Overcoming — 75
14. Knowing the Voice of God — 81
15. Test of Faith — 87
16. The Power of Words — 93
17. Digging Deeper — 99
18. What Are You Waiting For? — 103
19. Wrap-Up — 111

Other titles by this author — 115

1
Where I Found God

I was lying at the bottom of my walk-in closet floor, curled up in a fetal position, crying. It was the spring of 2011, and I was in my 30th year. All of my insecurities, low self-esteem, and bad choices had helped get me to this breaking point. Broken I was.

The choices that I had made leading up to this moment were largely affected by my childhood. Growing up, my mother constantly put me down with her words. Nothing I said or did was ever good enough. No matter how well I did my chores, no matter how good of grades that I got, it was never right or good enough. How I did my hair or what I wore was also analyzed and criticized on a regular basis. There was also no love or affection in our home.

After years of judgement, criticism, and rejection, I learned without realizing it how to withdraw from people in general. I put up a protective wall. If I wasn't noticed, then I couldn't be criticized. So I learned to stay in the back of a room in order to try to not be noticed.

I learned as an adult that I often avoided eye contact with people. Maybe it was because I didn't want them to engage me and find the things wrong with me that my mother seemed to find wrong with me.

I met a man in 2009 that had an effect on me that no one else had ever had. I will call him Chance. Chance lived in the same area of town as I did, near Memphis, Tennessee, and we were involved in some of the same things. I never saw him with a woman, yet I did see him with children, so I assumed that he was a single dad.

When I was around him, he had this way with words. He was very charming, and he made me feel better about myself than anyone ever had. He had a way of building me up and also making me feel comfortable. He was easy to talk to and also a great listener. He made me feel special. I found myself thinking about him a lot.

Then, I found out through social media that he was actually married. I felt guilty for having thought about him so much. I brushed the thoughts of him aside for almost a year. The

I Found God Outside of Church

following year, I received news regarding a family member going back into a bad home situation. This put me at a particular low. Guess who contacted me at that time? You guessed it: Chance. Although he had contacted me regarding a business matter, he started asking questions about what was going on, and I answered. One text led to another text to another text and another. The texting became more frequent. Before long, we agreed to meet up.

In a short period of time, we both opened up to each other quite a bit. I found out pretty soon that his marriage wasn't in good shape. They had been sleeping in separate rooms for several years. This helped me justify in my mind my getting into a relationship with him. I felt like I was single and not cheating on anyone. I also believed that things were basically over between them before I came along. That's what I told myself anyways.

I fell hard and fast. I wanted to be with and talk to Chance all the time. Although we spent a lot of time on the phone and in person together, it never seemed to be enough for me. He was like a drug for me. In a matter of months, Chance wanted me to sound out my first name with his last name. We talked of marriage and a family together. I wanted that with him. The connection I felt with him was more powerful than any I had ever had with another human being. It hurt to be apart from him.

Prior to this, I had always had walls up in all of my relationships. I didn't realize it though until the moment that they all came down. Somehow, in a matter of approximately 7 months, all of my walls came down with Chance. That was a true miracle for me to let anyone in at that level. It had taken 29 years for that moment to come. I didn't expect it or even know it was possible. For the first time, I could actually see myself having children. I could actually see this man in the delivery room with me. That was huge. I had never been able to get to that point before.

Growing up in Memphis, I was never the girl who talked about getting married and having three kids and a dog. I used to adamantly state as a teenager that I would never get married and that I would never have kids. It wasn't like I saw anything good regarding marriage and family growing up in my home, so why would I want something that was bad? Once you have a child with someone, that is not something that can be undone. That involved a level of trust that I couldn't fathom – until now anyways.

Of course, when a person feels truly loved and has a strong connection on every level, all of that can be thrown out the window. That's how it was with Chance. I had never connected with anyone like I connected with him. The relationship grew very quickly. We would talk for hours on end. The bond between us was very strong. We both seemed to share things with each other that we hadn't necessarily told anyone else. We went very deep, very fast. The entire relationship was intense.

In a short period of time, I came to a place where I seemed to need him in my life. I thrived on our communication and relationship. In fact, during the week of my birthday, I was on the phone with Chance one day at work. After my coworkers heard me on the phone with him, they said that I lit up when talking to him and that I should definitely spend my birthday with whoever was causing me to light up like that. Another time at a restaurant, the waitress called us "lovebirds." I think that she saw the way that I looked at him.

Without realizing it, I became emotionally dependent upon him. He seemed to want me to need him. He liked for me to turn to him when things would happen in my life that were difficult. He wanted to be a part of all that was going on with me, and I let him. Somehow, I seemed to lose any balance that I might have had prior to him coming into my life. I was consumed with him and anything and everything pertaining to him. Everything else seemed to be put on the back burner.

This relationship seemed to be what I was living for. It was like a drug. I was addicted to this man and the way that he made me feel. I never seemed to have enough time with him.

There was a fateful weekend in 2011. Just when I expected our relationship to go to the next level, something happened. Although he had signed a lease for his own place, when it came time for him to actually move, Chance had a change of heart. It happened so fast. It was like the flip of a light switch. It happened out of nowhere and was completely unexpected to me. All of the sudden, it was as though I didn't exist to him. It was as though the past 7 months hadn't happened. It felt like a

I Found God Outside of Church

bad dream, yet it wasn't.

He literally just stopped talking to me. Out of nowhere, once all of my walls were down, the very last thing I expected to happen, happened. We went from talking multiple times a day to it being as though we never knew each other. It was as though I wasn't even worth a text message to him. I was crushed.

Devastated, hurt, confused, struggling for breath – these words only begin to explain what I was feeling. I wasn't sure I knew what was real anymore. How could I have been sure enough about this person to have let all of my walls down and now this? I began to wonder how a person knows what's real in life. How do we really know if the sky is blue? How do we know that up is up and down is down? This shook me to my core.

How could I have seen myself having children with this person? I was left reeling in a way that I had never experienced before. I felt like I was disposable garbage to Chance. How could I have felt so loved, accepted, and wanted one minute and now this? This hit me out of nowhere it seemed. I didn't know what had hit me, but the pain was very real and very intense.

I had experienced rejection before but nothing like this. This cut in a way that nothing else ever had. During the relationship, I had been reassured over and over about our future together. I thought that I had asked every possible question. How did this happen?

He ignored my calls and texts initially. Eventually, I was able to hunt him down for answers, but talking to him only gave me more questions. There was no good answer that he could give that would give me peace. There was someone else that I would have to find for the answers that I really needed.

I remember talking to my best friend during this time. I think she got tired of hearing me talk about the same thing over and over again. Eventually, she pointed me to a Godly woman who had given her wise counsel in the past.

I was desperate for help, hope, and answers. I had never been at such a low place. Every-day functioning was hard. For the first time in my life, it felt like it took effort to simply breathe. I spent some time with the Godly woman, and she pointed me to the Bible. She gave me Scriptures to read and memorize. I was desperate for help, hope, and healing, and I gladly took all

Where I Found God

the advice I could get.

My pain was very intense. This was the most difficult season of my life. I had witnessed and experienced abuse in our home growing up. My father had died when I was 11 years old. But nothing had hurt me like this. It was so unexpected.

I had trouble sleeping. All I could seem to think about was how Chance had hurt me. I couldn't seem to find rest or peace. Every night as I would lay in my bed, I was tormented with thoughts of all that had transpired. The pain was real.

Not having him to talk to and share my daily life with was very hard for me. I didn't know how to continue without him. I had trouble remembering my life before him. I didn't understand how this had happened. I was a mess – a broken mess.

One day, I was driving down a main road in our city, and there he was. I spotted his truck immediately. Simply passing him on the road seemed to bring about some kind of emotional breakdown for me. The pain I felt was so intense. I remember getting home, pulling into my garage, sitting in my car, and just weeping. I couldn't seem to find the strength to get out of my car.

I cried every day during this season. I'm not sure how I got to work and was still able to do my job. That was truly a miracle considering the shape I was in.

One day, I was to the point of desperation. I was broken, and I wanted my pain to end. I ended up crying on the floor of my walk-in closet. I was at the lowest of lows. Then, it came to me: "Come to me, all of you who are weary and carry heavy burdens, and I will give you rest" (Matthew 11:28, NLT). It must have been one of the verses that the Godly woman had pointed me to. I cried out to God from a childlike state. I felt helpless. I told God through my tears that He said to come to Him if we have a heavy burden. And I could barely speak the words that my burden was so heavy. I told Him that I need the rest that He promises.

It's hard to explain the overwhelming peace and comfort that washed over me in that moment. My burden was immediately so much lighter. The circumstance was the same, but I was different. It's difficult to describe the presence of God if you haven't experienced it. It truly is something to be experienced. I could feel Him there with me. I could feel His love

I Found God Outside of Church

for me, and I knew that everything was going to be ok.

And that's where I found God – where I called out to Him from the bottom of my heart. I found Him at the bottom of my closet floor. He came to me.

Calling out to Him was one of the best decisions of my life. After feeling His love for me, it made it easier to continue to call out to Him. A very personal relationship of me going to Him daily began in that moment. I had read Scripture, had devotional books, and even listened to Christian music that was encouraging. I had been in church for years, but I had never experienced His love for me and His presence like this before. This personal encounter with God changed everything.

I had heard facts about God for years, but there was a disconnect in the relationship being personal. Now, when I went to church, it was more meaningful. I remember the next time we had communion and how deeply it moved me. I was beginning to understand at a higher level what Jesus had done on the Cross. He had this pain that I'm experiencing and a whole bunch more put on Him. That was difficult to fathom. At the same time, He not only had this put on Him, but He overcame. He overcame it all by rising from the dead 3 days later. This meant that I also could overcome.

The Cross became personal for me after the pain that I experienced in this season. It wasn't a fact that I heard about anymore; it was personal and relatable. It was something that I now understood through my own pain. What Jesus went through for us is not fully fathomable, but it is life-changing. I learned that there's something good that can come out of these moments where we feel like a big part of us has died. If we will invite God into that pain and brokenness, there's new life awaiting us on the other side of that "death."

Just when I felt like my life was over, it was really just beginning. In many ways, my life began in that moment. A transformation began in me. Years of low self-esteem and unhealthy relationship choices had led to this moment of complete brokenness. I found that God wanted to do something with my brokenness. He wasn't afraid to go into my hurt places and heal me and just love me. The love I experienced from Him was so powerful and unconditional. There was no mess too big for Him to handle, and trust me, I was a mess!

Where I Found God

I learned that my walls needed to be torn down through that relationship. Not only had I had walls up with others, but I had had walls up with God. I had trusted God in certain areas of my life and my heart before this, but I definitely had had at least one area that I hadn't trusted Him with: relationships. Interestingly, the one area that I wasn't trusting God in was the very area I experienced so much pain.

The problem with walls is that they not only block out bad things, but they also block out good things. I understand wanting to protect one's self from hurt. Unfortunately, walls will also protect you from good that's out there.

The one thing we withhold from God and don't surrender is the very thing that will cause the most pain in our lives. I started to learn that God never gave us rules or guidelines in the Bible because He doesn't want us to have any fun. I now began to understand that He wants to protect us from harm. That's why He says not to do certain things. He sees ahead and knows the results. It's just like a parent that doesn't want their child to run out into the street. The parent knows that there's potential harm there. It's not that the parent is trying to withhold fun from their child. It's the same with God.

How deceived I had been for so many years in a "Christian" church and also in a "Christian" school. I never understood the love of God. It truly is the love of God that changes everything. His love enabled me to let Him into all of those places within me that needed healing and transformation that I didn't even know that I needed healing in.

Understanding how God wanted the very best for me was huge. Understanding how He accepted me in whatever condition I was in was huge. Understanding that I was good enough for His love was also huge.

Getting free was a process for me. Freedom was not instantaneous. The peace that God gave was instantaneous though. I was still in a battle. I still found myself wanting to talk to Chance. I knew within me that the relationship had involved sexual sin, but also my emotions seemed so tied to him that it was very hard to break free.

Mentally, it was hard not to think about him. It was hard to not reach out to him. I did still reach out to him some. Sometimes, when you're going forward, you may take a few

I Found God Outside of Church

steps back. Sometimes, this is part of the journey and how you learn and grow. God was so faithful to me in this season. He didn't judge me. He didn't scold me. He loved me through this time. Love was what I needed. Love made me comfortable to be real with God.

God also put two important women in my life at the time. Prior to this time in my life, I had never had a friend that I could be 100% real with. My best friend Nicole was the one person that I could share everything with and know that I wouldn't be judged. She may not have agreed with all of my decisions, but she was there for me and didn't judge me. That was huge. She was such a huge support to me during this time. She was like an angel to me.

The particular weekend that everything came crashing down in the relationship, I knew that I shouldn't be alone. The thoughts that can come to a person who feels crushed, devastated, hopeless, and worthless are not good. I had had these types of thoughts of giving up come to me before, and I knew that I didn't need to be alone.

It was hard for me to ask to stay with Nicole, but I knew I needed to. I slept on her couch that weekend when I was in such a weak state. If it weren't for her, I don't think I would've been able to get up and get in the shower that weekend. I was so weak.

I still remember her making breakfast for us. She made this huge omelet for me. I probably wouldn't have eaten that day if it weren't for her. I felt the love behind the omelet. It was as though I had reverted to a childlike state, yet I could safely expose this to her. That was huge. I had never had that kind of friendship with anyone before her. God truly put her in my life.

Also, there was the Godly woman that Nicole had directed me to: Linda. Linda had a great impact on my life in this season. She would pray with me, love me, and point me even further to God. She gave me Scriptures to meditate on and resources to go to. I was like a sponge. I was hungry for all the help that was available to me. God used her as an integral part of my journey of spiritual growth and healing. God will put the right people in your life during these times. These two women I will forever be grateful for.

I struggled to move past this relationship and move on with

my life. Running into Chance a couple of times after this was almost more than I could bare. God is so amazing. He knew just what I needed.

A year prior to this, I had put in an application for a different job locally but didn't get it. Now, that same organization is contacting me regarding a job opportunity with them in Savannah, Georgia. Getting far away from Chance seemed to be something that I needed to do in order to really heal and move forward.

When I was at my worst and coming out of the deepest sin that I had ever been in and reaping the pain from that sin, God showed up and rescued me. This opportunity to get away and work for an amazing organization with great benefits in Savannah, Georgia, was definitely a gift from God. On top of that, I would be less than 30 minutes from the beach!

Before I continue this part of the story, I want to share with you some of my church experiences that I had had leading up to this point. Unfortunately, many of them weren't good, especially in my teen years.

2
Bad Church Experiences

What type of church experiences have you had? Have you had any bad ones? I've had quite a few.

I grew up in a family that went to church every time the doors were open. Going to church wasn't optional. I also was in "Christian" schools from Kindergarten through 12th grade. Through all of those years, I associated God with strict rules, no fun, and judgement. Once I got into my teen years, I remember thinking that I didn't want to end up with a "good Christian man" in terms of marriage. My view of "good Christians" wasn't very good. I didn't think that I was good enough to be with a "good Christian." I also didn't think that they really enjoyed life.

I mostly heard what you shouldn't do and can't do. Anyone who didn't follow the many rules was judged harshly and talked about negatively. Outsiders weren't warmly welcomed as far as I could see. I didn't feel that I measured up or was good enough to fit in with "good Christians." Why would I want to be around people who make me feel bad about myself?

Also, everything was very controlled – where you couldn't go, what you couldn't do, what music you couldn't listen to, what you couldn't wear, etc. There were very few things that were acceptable.

I still remember the way that one church member was looked at, talked about, and treated after he went through a divorce. It was as though he couldn't be trusted anymore or was a different person. New people to the church were also looked at suspiciously.

Although I can recall some kind, loving people growing up in church, it was hard to ignore all of the negative things that I experienced and to separate all of the bad apart from my view of God. I didn't know that there was any reason to separate the two.

As I said, my family went to church every time the doors were open. I was the third of four girls. I had two older sisters and one younger. My dad had died when I was 11 years old from cancer. In my teen years, my older two sisters had already moved out, so it was just me, my mom, and my youngest sister

I Found God Outside of Church

at home.

In church, at school, and at home, I heard a lot about all of the things that you shouldn't do. I heard a lot of condemnation and judgement. "Don't, don't, and don't" seemed to be common themes in the church. I didn't think that Christians really had any fun. I also experienced a lot of gossip, judgement, and criticism towards myself or anyone else who didn't follow all of the many rules. It seemed that many at church were always suspicious, judging, and condemning. I felt like church was something that we went to because others would think badly of us if we didn't.

I had a number of bad experiences in the church that I was brought up in. Several of these happened when I was a teenager. When I was 13 or 14, the church youth group announced that they would be taking a mission trip to Mexico. I had grown up in a strict home and rarely got to do anything, so I was extremely excited about the idea of getting to travel to another country.

I worked very hard over a period of several months in order to be able to go on the trip. We completed a bunch of weekly assignments that had points attached. If you earned enough points at the end, the church would cover the cost for you to go on the trip. The only personal cost was spending money.

I was very motivated. This was something to look forward to. They also were stopping in Texas and going to a Six Flags theme park on the way. I was excited and quickly calculated what was necessary to be able to go.

Not only did I work hard to be able to go, but I also worked with my good friend each week and helped her with the assignments so that she could go too. I would go to her house or have her come to mine and help her learn the Scripture for the week. This went on for months. I was very determined and very motivated. Not only did I earn enough points for the trip, but I ended up with the most points. They presented me with a Bible as my reward in front of the church. My friend also ended up with enough points to go. I was ecstatic.

When it came down to the actual trip, I was in for some real disappointment. They decided to make the dress code even stricter than it already was. They had already warned us that there would be no air conditioning where we would be staying.

Bad Church Experiences

It was summertime. They now tell us that we can't wear sleeveless tops. That was only the beginning. When we got to Texas, they were talking harshly to us and treating us like we were bad kids who couldn't be trusted. I hadn't expected this. We had worked so hard all year for this. There was a meanness that was unnecessary.

The facility that we stayed in in Mexico was a large room with a bunch of bunk beds. The guys were in a separate room. We referred to one female leader on the trip as "Sergeant Carter." She was like a military machine. She was so strict and so mean. She told us that we could only take two-minute showers. There was no reason stated for why the showers needed to be only two minutes. How many American women, especially teenagers, do you know who can do all they need to do with a two-minute shower? This was a problem. It took me almost that long just to get my long hair wet. I literally had to skip breakfast so that I could take a shower and do everything that I needed to do without someone yelling for me to get out.

This definitely wasn't what I expected after working so hard all year. They also seemed to be analyzing what we were wearing with a microscope. It was hard to shake all of the negativity from leadership. They didn't treat us or talk to us in a way that conveyed that we were good kids, had worked hard all year for this trip, and could be trusted.

There were several other bad experiences connected to this same church in my teen years. One involved a trip to St. Louis. After we returned from the trip, it was discovered by church leadership that several of the guys and girls were holding hands and kissing on the trip. One of the leaders told us very harshly that he would never take us anywhere again. I still remember this over twenty years later. I can't help but wonder if that same leader held hands, kissed, or broke any rules as a teenager.

Another time when I was 15 or 16, one of the youth leaders yelled at my boyfriend in front of the group and accused us of being up to something on the church van. We were on separate seats and not doing anything. It seemed like we were always surrounded by suspicion. I remember never wanting to go back. The way that he talked to us was humiliating.

One night, one of the church members told my mom that my boyfriend (same guy from previous story) and I were making

I Found God Outside of Church

out in the parking lot. He wasn't even at church that night. Do people not have anything better to do than to make up lies?

Interestingly enough, those statements and accusations seemed to become self-fulfilling prophecies. We did end up doing a lot of things at church that embarrass me now to look back on. If they were going to say that we were always up to something, we may as well have been.

In my adult years, after experiencing the love and presence of God after the situation with Chance, I eventually began serving in church. And yes, I still had more bad church experiences.

I was in one church that supported a local mission that helped people coming out of addictions, homelessness, prison, etc. Although the financial support to the mission sounds good on the surface, the actual treatment of the guys when they came to the church wasn't always great. The church had guys from this mission work in their parking lot to direct traffic on Sunday mornings. These guys didn't volunteer to help. They were told they had to. Some of them complained to me that they didn't want to miss Sunday school or the worship songs in church while directing the traffic in the parking lot. When a new guy would come to the mission and first come to the church, they were immediately told to work in the parking lot. Some of these guys had never been to church before. Their first church experience involved being told to go outside and help. They were forced to serve. The very people who needed serving the most were forced to serve the rest of the congregation.

This reminds me of a story in the Bible where it talks about Jesus overturning tables of moneychangers in the temple (John 2:13-17). Although the two circumstances are very different, I believe that this situation would also anger Jesus to action. The church should be a place where the hurting find help, not where they are forced to help. Some things going on in churches don't reflect God at all.

The Bible says that what we do to the least of these, we do to Jesus. I don't consider these guys to be the least, but many in the culture would. In that case, this church made Jesus work in the parking lot when He arrived! It's a disgrace. It was almost as though these guys owed the church something for the church supporting the mission.

Bad Church Experiences

Some things going on in churches today are the farthest thing from reflecting the heart of God and who He really is. What's the point in sending money to that organization if you're going to treat them this way? How are you helping them spiritually? How are you pointing them to God? Are you in fact turning them away from God? This is a problem.

I've had others share some of their bad church experiences with me. One man that I met, who was brought up in the Catholic church, doesn't want any more to do with God or the church because of the sexual abuse that several priests were convicted of. Another man was in a church where it was found out that the pastor had been stealing money from the church, so he turned away from God and the church.

I faced many spiritual attacks when teaching an adult Sunday school class. One guy had befriended me from the very first night I showed up at this particular church. I thought of him as a supportive, Christian friend. However, the minute I signed up to teach this class, I saw a whole new side to this person.

A couple days before I was to teach at the church for the first time, I was on the phone with him. I heard the Lord telling me to not engage, yet it seemed hard to not answer a question when he asked. This guy starts asking me if I believe the Bible in its entirety. I could tell by the tone of his voice that he didn't mean well. He seemed angry that I was going to teach. He seemed to have a problem with me being a woman and the class being co-ed. He berated me. I hadn't expected this from him of all people. I thought he was a friend.

Jealousy is another issue that I've faced when serving in church. God specifically directed me to this particular church and Sunday school class to serve in. When I started teaching there, all of the sudden several other people wanted to start teaching in that same class. They didn't seem to want to do this until I arrived. One woman on the church staff seemed to be particularly jealous of me. At one point she said to me somewhat rudely, "Where did you come from?" She acted like she felt threatened by me. Maybe the devil deceived her and made her think that I wanted her position on the church staff. Who knows? Aren't we supposed to be on the same team here? Why aren't you happy that God has sent someone who wants to help share the load?

I Found God Outside of Church

On another occasion, someone decided to change the teaching schedule for the class. That same woman came to me right before class started to tell me that I had been put down to teach that day. I don't know if there was malice behind the way it was handled, but I said that it was no problem and went on with teaching the class with no lesson prepared. I sensed that this woman hoped that I would fail in some way.

I never told the class that I didn't have anything prepared or that I was given no notice. I just let God lead me and the class. Later, someone from the class told me that it was one of the best classes he had ever been in.

Another time, God told me to leave the church I was in. I was very involved in the church, and I gave them two weeks' notice. The pastor seemed to take it very personally that I was leaving. With malice in his eyes, he told me very hatefully that he was removing me from the areas of the church I was serving in for the remaining time. There was no reason given, other than the fact that I hadn't told him why I was leaving.

Pastors aren't God. Pastors are also not perfect. And frankly, some pastors that have the title of "pastor" have that title from man, not necessarily from God. Not everyone who is working in a particular position at a church has actually been called by God to do what they are doing. And unfortunately, not all serving in churches have pure motives.

Stories of bad church experiences are varied and vast. Of course, churches are made up of people, and the only kind of people there are are imperfect ones. This includes me. Christians aren't perfect, and some who claim to be Christians aren't. Some who appear to be working for God are actually helping turn people away from God.

There's an important fact that helps explain why there are so many bad church experiences: Satan. Satan is real, and one of his favorite hangouts is the church. Satan is the opposite of everything good. He hangs out in churches because he doesn't want you to know that God is good. He wants you to have a bad experience and to think that the experience was from God. He then hopes to turn you away from God. He doesn't want you to find God or help. He doesn't want you to find truth that will set you free.

Satan works through deception. He deceived the very first

man and woman, and he's still up to the same thing. If he can inflict something bad on you and make you think it was from God and not him, then he can try to persuade you to turn away from God. He's succeeded in doing this with many.

Satan is very strategic. He wants you to have a bad church experience so that you will then turn away from God. Please know that when you go to church, Satan doesn't want you there. You have a true enemy. Although you can't see him physically, if you look, you'll see the things that he's behind. He'll try to push your buttons and offend you through other people there, and yes, it may even be by the pastor or someone else on the church staff. If this happens, there must be something good there for you that Satan doesn't want you to have. Don't let him deceive you or steal from you.

Other accusations and lies have come at me. Once, a man in the Sunday school class where I taught went to church leadership and told them that one of the other men in the class had some sort of sexual relationship with me and that this man was going around telling people about these supposed sexual acts. I got word of this rumor, and God gave me such peace. I knew that these were lies. The Word of God says that no weapon that forms against God's servants will prosper. In other words, things will form and come against them, but nothing will come of them, unless they allow them to.

When the man who made these accusations was questioned further by church leadership, he admitted that he had "heard a voice telling him to go to those specific people and tell them what he had told them." He admitted lying. Interestingly, I had already had other attacks come at me through the very church leaders that this voice / the devil told him to go to. This didn't surprise me too much.

Later, the pastor told me a vague overview of what had happened. I was never even questioned by him. The truth came out before it could get to that point. He seemed to feel badly for me because the rumors were vicious. He didn't even want to repeat them. I didn't need any details, as I know that the devil is a liar. I don't need any of his lies trying to steal my joy or stick to me. I never asked any questions about the incident, and I continued to teach in the class.

There were other attacks too, but I think you get the point.

I Found God Outside of Church

The truth is that people were getting saved and finding hope, help, and freedom. The truth was going out, and people's lives were being changed in that class. That's why the devil spent so much time and energy trying to come after me. I truly enjoyed teaching that class. I grew through each attack and gained spiritual insight too.

It's very important to understand that there's only one perfect man; His name is Jesus. At any time, any person, even good people, can be used by Satan in a weak moment. We must follow Jesus. He must be our ultimate example. Yes, it's good to be mentored and to learn from others, but realize that people are just people. Just because someone has a title or is in church leadership, this doesn't make them perfect, sinless, or incapable of falling or being used by the devil.

I've met many people that have had a bad church experience. In fact, I don't know that I've met anyone that hasn't had a bad experience at church at some point in time or another. Satan uses people. If one of the twelve disciples that walked closely with Jesus could be used by Satan, then so can anyone else. I'm referring to a man named Peter. Jesus said to Peter, "Get behind Me, Satan" (Matthew 16:23, NKJV)! Jesus was talking to a person, but obviously, that person was being used by Satan in that moment.

I've also found that one of the ways that God likes us to grow is through opposition – those who are against us or at least seem to be. Each time that I faced opposition and didn't run from it, I learned much and came out much stronger than before.

If you've gone to church and had a bad church experience, you're not alone. If you've quit going to church or are thinking of not going, I can understand. However, that's exactly what Satan hopes you will do. Spiritual battles are real. Although you see a person in front of you, you're dealing with whatever spirit or spirits that he or she is yielded to in his or her life.

I've faced many spiritual attacks in churches, and many of them have come from people who are paid at the church to do the work of God. This is sad, but the truth is that when you are exactly where you're supposed to be and doing exactly what God calls you to do, you will face opposition. Read in Scripture about Jesus and the opposition that He faced from the "religious" people.

I had one person say to me when something came against me, "It's not personal." In one sense, he was right. It's not personal, but it is spiritual, which frankly feels worse than when it's just personal. You're dealing with evil spirits that hate you and don't want you to be where God wants you to be. And they definitely don't want you helping anyone else in the church.

I've learned to try to take it as a compliment when things come at me. I must be doing something right if the devil is coming after me.

After all of these negative experiences, you may be wondering why in the world I would still want to go to church and encourage you to do the same. Although I've shared a lot of bad experiences with you, these experiences were spread out over many years and different churches. Not all of my church experiences have been bad. I've also had very positive and rewarding experiences at church that far outweigh the bad. I'll share some of those with you in a later chapter.

For now, let's get back to the story. What would happen if I moved away from Chance and away from family and friends to a new state where I knew no one?

3
The Worst Thing and the Best Thing

Moving to a new city and state more than 600 miles from home isn't always an easy thing to do. Yet, that's exactly what I did in September 2011. The journey from Memphis, Tennessee, to Savannah, Georgia, would be an interesting one to say the least. Many unknowns lay ahead.

Pain has an interesting way of causing a person to make decisions that they otherwise wouldn't make. If I hadn't gone through what I did, I don't think that I would've accepted a new job and moved. Learning where the gas station, grocery store, and Taco Bell were located were major priorities. Getting situated in my new apartment didn't turn out to be a simple task either. A cord had to be changed on my clothes dryer before it could be plugged into the wall. Although the man at the hardware store was very helpful, I still electrocuted myself in the process. Leave these things to the professionals, folks.

I knew absolutely zero people in Georgia. It was literally just me and God on this journey. I'm pretty sure that that was part of the point of me moving. Sometimes, the hardest thing to do is also the best thing to do. Although it was very hard to leave certain family members (especially my nephew) when I moved, I also knew that it was the right and best thing for me to do at that time.

That first year, particularly that first Christmas, was very hard for me. Being away from family, friends, and all I had ever known was not very enjoyable. I was now having to face some things within myself that I otherwise might not have dealt with.

It was December 2011. I had been living in Savannah, Georgia, for only three months. I had no close friends or family in the area. I had moved with a broken heart. I had made choices to live in sin and had reaped the consequences.

Moving away was necessary in order for me to be able to really move forward with my life. I was struggling to let go of Chance. Even after I moved, I struggled with thoughts of him daily. For many months, I cried daily. The thing about pain is that even if you get away from the situation that caused the pain, the pain that you feel still goes with you wherever you go.

I Found God Outside of Church

I had one television, which I set up in my apartment living room. I learned that sometimes quiet can be too quiet. That was the case for me when I first arrived in Savannah. The dark and quiet nights were too dark and too quiet in my bedroom, so for the first few months, I slept on my couch in the living room in order to have the television on. It's strange how our habits can change with different seasons.

This was a lonely season for me. Moving to a new city had been almost overwhelming for me in the emotional condition that I was in. It seemed to take all the strength that I had to get a few presents in the mail for family before Christmas that year. I was exhausted and very down. I had had very different expectations than my current reality. I had thought that I would be with the man that I loved this Christmas. Here I was in another state, feeling all alone and miserable. Sin will definitely leave you with a very different outcome than you want, expect, or anticipate.

Through social media I had reconnected with a girl I had known in middle school. She was now a single mom going through a difficult time. I was at home one evening when God began to give me thoughts of doing something for her this Christmas. I was so tired though. I didn't feel that I had any extra energy for anyone else. I felt like I was doing good to take care of myself at this point. God gave me the idea of getting her a gift card. Although this might sound like a small and simple thing, I felt too tired and too weak to go to the store and find time to go to the post office yet again. God continued to give me this idea until I gave in and went. I sent it in the mail and didn't think much more about it.

Then, there was one family member that I had debated on what to get her and how much to spend on her this Christmas. Sometimes, it's easier to do things for people whom you are closer with. This family member can be the challenging one, the one that can cause a scene at family gatherings. I'm not proud of the fact that I didn't really want to spend as much on this family member. I remember God saying to me, "So, you're praying for this person to get delivered, yet you don't want to give to her?" It didn't make sense to withhold from someone who was probably more in need than the rest of us. So, I sent her two gift cards; one was for a grocery store.

The Worst Thing and the Best Thing

The week of Christmas came, and I was at such a low point. I was bitter towards the man who had played a big part in me being in this state. I was feeling sorry for myself since I would be spending Christmas basically alone. I was upset with myself for believing and trusting all that this man had told me. I was a mess. I would come home from work and not eat anything. Not even food could help the way that I was feeling. I wanted nothing. It seemed that nothing could help my current situation. A couple of gifts came in the mail, and I immediately tore them open. I was looking for some kind of relief or something to lift my spirits, but I was still empty after I opened them. I had reached a new level of miserable.

I was on my way home from work one night a few days before Christmas, and I received a message from the single mom. Her words pierced my heart. She had received the gift card and said that she knew that God had put me in her life and that I was like an angel to her. She said that she couldn't express what it meant to her to be able to now do something for her kids this Christmas. I was amazed. I had forgotten all about that gift card that I had struggled to send.

I was so thankful now that God had persistently nudged me to do this until I actually did it. To think that I almost didn't do this. What if I had withheld this from her? I was thankful that God was able to use me. I thought to myself, "Ok, this time of year isn't about me. It's about others." This did help lift my spirits. To think that God was trying to help ME by asking me to do this. He knew the condition that I would be in this week.

That same week, I got a message from the challenging family member. She tells me that she had needed to get three things from the grocery store, but she only had $5. She said that she doesn't usually get the mail every day, but for some reason, she got the mail that day, and there was the grocery store gift card that I had sent. Now, she was able to get everything that she needed and still have money left over. This blew me away. To think that I almost didn't do this either. I was glad now that I had listened to God. Even though I was so down, I was glad that He was able to use me in some small way to be a blessing to someone else.

But I was still struggling mentally and emotionally. I wanted this season to be over with. Someone from my church had a

I Found God Outside of Church

group over on Christmas Eve. I brought a Christmas Bible trivia game. It's basically questions about the time around Jesus' birth that most people are not familiar with. I brought a bag of candy, and each time someone got a question right, they got to choose from the bag any item that they liked. Everyone had a great time with it. It was interesting that I was able to help others have a good time when I was so miserable on the inside. It was good to get out of the house though and get my mind off of things. However, those things still awaited me once I was alone with my thoughts again.

I woke up Christmas morning alone and with no presents to open, since I had already opened the ones that had come. It dawned on me that I had thought about going to the beach to see the sunrise over the ocean Christmas morning since I wouldn't have anything else to do. It seemed like it was already light outside. Oh no! I bet I missed the sunrise since I didn't set my alarm! I quickly searched online for "sunrise Tybee Island." This is the name of the nearby beach. I learned that the official sunrise would take place in 20 minutes. I knew that I needed to hurry in order to not miss it.

I quickly got dressed and put on a coat and gloves. I then grabbed my camping chair and devotional book and headed out. As I'm driving towards the beach, I realize that the sky is very overcast. There are very thick, low-lying clouds in the sky. Great, now I won't even be able to see the sunrise with these thick clouds. I was already complaining and feeling like this was a total waste of my time.

I got to the beach and set my camping chair up and just sat there amongst the ocean breeze and the sounds of the crashing waves. I began to reflect on everything that had happened in my life that led me to move to another state and to be spending this Christmas alone. I felt frustrated that I wasn't even getting to see the one thing that I wanted to see that morning – the sunrise over the ocean.

As I was sitting there, all of the sudden, God spoke to me: "You're focused on the wrong sun." The Son! All this time I had been so focused on myself. Then, I had thought that this time of year should be about other people. The Son, Jesus, had definitely not been my focus at all. Sure, I had heard the saying and probably even quoted it: "Jesus is the reason for the

The Worst Thing and the Best Thing

season." But that statement was far from my reality.

I was humbled by these words. Hearing this was so freeing. When we hear and know the truth, it really does set us free. As I was processing that, God spoke again and said: "And Satan used you too." All this time, I had been bitter towards the man who had hurt me, and it seemed so clear to me how Satan had used him in my life. But now, God was telling me that I was not innocent and that Satan had used me too. This also helped set me free. I needed to hear that. I needed to stop blaming Chance. It's always so easy to see how others are wrong. It's not so easy to own our own responsibility in things. There truly is none righteous, no, not one (Romans 3:10).

The presence of God there with me was unlike anything I have ever experienced. It took so much to get me to that moment in my life where everything else was drowned out so that I could hear Him clearly. Oh, how I needed this. I just sat there crying good tears. My perspective and focus had been all wrong. It took me some time to reflect on what I had just heard.

Eventually, I wiped my tears and my nose and got up to take a walk. I felt so much better now. I felt lighter. I felt freer. I felt silly for being so upset about the sunrise. As I walked along the edge of the water, suddenly, I felt this intense warmth on the back of my coat. As I turned around to see what it was, I was almost blinded by a light from the sky. I just stood there with my eyes squinted, soaking it in, and I began to cry again. It felt like God Himself was shining down on me from heaven. It left me frozen to that spot, to that moment in time, unable to speak or move. All I could do was soak it in. Crying was the only way to express the incredible emotions that I was feeling. It was like God literally peeled back the thick cloud where I was standing in order to shine down upon me. He did this just for me. Words can't explain the power of this moment. Eventually, I began to walk again. What a day!

This Christmas started as the worst Christmas of my life. I had never experienced so much pain on any other Christmas. But then, I had this amazing encounter with God that changed everything. What started as the worst Christmas turned into the best Christmas of my life. It's strange that both the best thing and the worst thing can be wrapped up in one, but that's exactly the way it is sometimes.

I Found God Outside of Church

In one sense, Jesus dying a very cruel death on a Cross is the best thing for us since it gives us the opportunity to have our sins forgiven, a personal relationship with God, and eternal life. At the same time, the fact that He was brutally tortured by the very people that He came to save is the worst thing. Somehow, both of these two facts are wrapped up in one. It's strange yet true that sometimes the best thing and the worst thing are the same thing.

If I was offered a million dollars or the experience that I had that Christmas morning on the beach, I would easily choose my experience. The one word that best describes that first Christmas in Savannah, both the worst and the best Christmas of my life, is priceless. God speaking to me that Christmas wouldn't be the last time that I would hear from Him.

4

Passing Him By

Amy's words pierced my heart. As I sat in my chair in our weekly Bible study, I listened to one of the women in the group tell a story. She was driving home one day after work when she saw a homeless man holding a sign asking for help near the stoplight. She saw him, but she didn't want to look at him. It made her uncomfortable. She felt a tug on her heart that she described as a weight on her chest to help him, but she thought, "What if he's an alcoholic? What if he wants money for drugs? What if he tries to carjack my car? Is he really even hungry? Is it safe to stop?" As she sat there, the weight on her chest continued. She knew that God wanted her to help him.

She had to make a quick decision. She looked around in her car and saw that she had a granola bar. She hesitantly rolled down the window and said, "Sir, all I have is this granola bar, but you're welcome to it." He gratefully accepted the granola bar, tore it open, and quickly devoured it right in front of her. She was shocked by what she saw. She then looked around and saw that she also had a bottle of water in the floor and a little change in her console. She reached out her window and gave him those things too. She realized that he wasn't just hungry; he was starving. She felt horrible for questioning his need. She had almost passed him by.

The stoplight turned green, and as she drove away, she saw in her rearview mirror that the person behind her was now giving the man something too. She was humbled and convicted. I was too, as I heard this story. How many times had I thought those same things? How had I misjudged countless others? God totally wanted to change her thinking, and He had. Her story resonated strongly with me. I had passed by many homeless people and thought similar things. I now knew that I had been wrong in my thinking and that the next time that I saw a homeless person, I should stop to help.

One night after work, I was on my way to the Christian bookstore when I noticed a homeless man holding a sign at the stoplight. Somewhere within me, I knew that I needed to help him, but I had other plans for the evening. I tried to think of

I Found God Outside of Church

where I could get some fast food for him, since I didn't want to give him money. I was in the downtown area and didn't know of anywhere close by that had a drive-through. This was an inconvenience.

I headed towards the Christian bookstore and remembered that there was a McDonald's close to the bookstore. I decided that I would get what I needed from the bookstore and then get some food for this man and bring it back to him.

When I got to the bookstore, I started questioning whether or not I should go back to the homeless man. I realized that by the time that I got the food and got back to him, almost an hour or more would have passed. He probably won't even be there anymore. This will be a waste of my time and out of my way too.

As I finished in the bookstore, I remembered telling God that I would help the next person that I saw in need. I knew it was the right thing to do. My friend's story had greatly impacted me. I knew that I needed to act after what I had heard. After wavering back and forth and trying to talk myself out of it, I decided to go to McDonald's to get the man some food.

The McDonald's that I went to had just added a second lane for ordering in the drive-through. After ordering, the two lanes merge into one. I placed the order in the second line and pulled forward to merge into the main line to get the food. The vehicle next to me finished ordering after me, yet they decided to quickly cut in front of me. The woman smiles at me as she is cutting in front of my vehicle. Seriously? I'm trying to get food for a homeless man. Then, to top it off, she has a bumper sticker from a local Christian church on her vehicle.

All I'm trying to do is get food for the homeless man, but this entails more than I expect. I'm having to overcome many things within myself. I think that God must have a sense of humor. Although the woman went to the trouble that she did to cut in front of me, her food wasn't ready when she got to the window. She had to pull forward and wait. Meanwhile, I got my food and left before she did.

Now, I have the food, but I immediately am questioning whether or not I should go back to this man. It's been an hour, and now, it's even started raining. I'm sure that he won't be there. This whole thing is pointless. I begin to think that this food is going to go to waste. Also, it's out of my way to go back through the downtown area before going home. There's a battle raging within me: do what I'm used to doing (nothing) and stay comfortable or get uncomfortable and do what I know is the right thing.

I decide to head back towards downtown. I approach the area and look to see if anyone is there. To my complete amazement, the same man is standing in the exact same spot that I left him! I'm speechless. I can't believe what I'm seeing. I drive towards him and have no idea what to say. This is way out of my comfort zone. I approach the light, roll down my window, and offer the food, which he gladly accepts. I tell him that God will help him get on his feet. He thanks me. The light quickly turns green, and I drive away.

So many things are running through my mind as I pull away. Before I have a chance to process what just happened, a beautiful half of a rainbow appears in the sky directly in front of me. I'm flooded with emotions. I can sense that God is with me and is pleased with me. It seems like the Lord Himself put this rainbow in the sky just for me. It's an overwhelming sensation. On the radio, a Christian song called "Light Up the Sky" by The Afters comes on. It describes exactly what I'm feeling in that moment.

Tears begin to stream down my face. To think that I almost didn't go back to him. I almost missed this opportunity. I thought I knew best, and I was wrong. What if I hadn't gone back? How long had he stood there? How many people had passed him by? How hard was it for him to stand out there begging? How hard was it when people didn't even want to look at him? How much did it hurt for so many cars to pass him by? What did it feel like knowing that these people would go home to an abundance yet refuse to even look at him, much less help him? What else had I been wrong about?

God later told me that the same is often true of how people feel looking at pictures or movies of Jesus on the Cross. People don't want to watch or embrace it too much because it makes them uncomfortable. Yet, how much more uncomfortable was it for Jesus to actually go through it? So many things are connected. God used this homeless man to give me greater insight into what Jesus endured.

I Found God Outside of Church

My next encounter was in the spring of 2012, not too long after the rainbow story. I had had my worst day on my job by far. I had had an expectation of getting a raise. When that didn't happen, I felt devastated. I had really been pouring myself into the work and had gone above and beyond what was asked or expected.

After work, I decided that I needed to get some take-out food as though maybe this would help me feel better. For some reason, I was craving shrimp fried rice. I was still new to the area and didn't know where to go for shrimp fried rice. I asked a coworker, and he told me an area where a shopping center was. I got there and didn't see a Chinese restaurant. Great! All I want is shrimp fried rice, and even that can't seem to happen easily. I was down, frustrated, and feeling empty and alone.

I got on my phone and searched for "Chinese restaurants" in the zip code of the area that I thought I was in. A Chinese restaurant popped up, and it was very close to where I was. In fact, it was directly across the street in another shopping center.

I pulled into the lot. All I wanted to do was get my food, go home, eat, and do absolutely nothing, except maybe feel sorry for myself. I was ready for this day to be over. As I got out of my car, I noticed a man sitting on the concrete sidewalk right outside the door to the Chinese restaurant. He was holding a sign asking for help. I walked by him and went into the restaurant.

As soon as I got inside, I heard the Lord say to me, "Did you see him?" I said in my head / to God, "Yes, but I've got my own problems right now." I ordered my food, and then, I heard again, "Did you see him?" Talking to a homeless man was the last thing that I wanted to do in that moment. I had my own issues, and I just wanted to be by myself. It seemed to take all the strength I had left, but I reluctantly went outside.

I had no idea what to say, so I simply asked him if he wanted to come inside and get something to eat. He said yes and followed me inside. This was way out of my comfort zone. As we were walking inside, I heard a phone ring. He reached into his backpack and pulled out a cell phone. I thought to myself, "I'm going to ignore that." Thoughts of, "If he can afford a cell phone, why can't he afford food?" started to come to my mind. Then, I thought I smelled alcohol on him. No, I'm going

Passing Him By

to ignore that too. Basically, after my friend's story, I knew that there was no good reason not to help someone if I had the means to do so. As we approached the counter, I told him that he could order anything he wanted. I then heard him order shrimp fried rice. I told him that was exactly what I had ordered.

We stood there waiting for our food, and it felt awkward. I didn't know what to say. This whole thing was awkward for me. I thought about inviting him to my church, but if he's homeless and has no transportation, it would be way too far for him to walk from this part of town. I told him that if he's ever in the area, he's welcome to visit our church.

Then, he asks me if I will pray for him. As in, he wants me to pray for him right there at the Chinese take-out counter. Umm, I wasn't expecting this. I definitely have never done anything like this before. I say yes and ask him what his first name is. I don't recall now what it was. I close my eyes and begin to pray for him out loud. As I do, I feel his hand on my shoulder. This is bizarre. I'm standing at the Chinese take-out counter, praying for this homeless man, while his hand is now on my shoulder. Strange doesn't describe the moment well enough.

I say a simple prayer asking God to help him get on his feet. I finish the prayer, and then, we get our food. I wish him well and take my food to my car to go home. When I get in my car, I begin to cry. I was feeling so sorry for myself and my situation, and here was someone who didn't even know where his next meal was coming from. I'm upset about not getting a raise; what if I didn't even have a job? I was humbled to say the least.

Suddenly, I felt so much better and lighter. It took me some time to get myself together in that parking lot. When I had gone into the restaurant, I was so burdened and down. Now, although my situation hadn't changed, my perspective had. I thought that I was going to bless the man by buying him a meal, but he had blessed me.

Sometime later, I had a very different experience. I was driving down a main highway to church and saw a man walking with a backpack on the side of the road. He looked clean-cut and stood out. I only saw him for a brief moment. I had a sense that I should stop and ask him if he needed help or a ride, but it happened so quickly. I passed him by. I had a tugging on my

I Found God Outside of Church

heart that I should turn around and go back to him, but I was lazy and disobedient. I was ready to get where I was going.

I continued on my journey and arrived to church. People were sharing testimonies, and we were having a great time. About 30-45 minutes later, the door opens, and in walks the man that I had passed on the road.

He shares that he's a Christian and feels led to travel around and share the news of Christ wherever God leads him. I sat there feeling horrible. I knew that I should have stopped, but I ignored the prompting. This man walked all that way when I literally had driven right past him. And now, I learn that he's a minister too. Conviction isn't a strong enough word to explain what I was feeling.

I wasn't sure how far he had walked before I had seen him either. The night went on, and I asked God if there was anything else I should do to help this man. God told me that I should ask him what he needed and provide whatever it was that he needed. I began to think, "What if he needs a place to stay for the night?" I mentioned that to God, and again, I heard that I should provide whatever he needs.

So, as we finished, I asked the man if there was anything that he needed. Sure enough, he said that he needed a place to stay for the night. Up to this point, I've pulled over many times and blessed people, but I had never invited anyone into my home for the night.

After having rejected what God had said the first time, how could I say no now? I told the man that he was welcome to stay at my place if he needed to for the night.

Although I was doing this, I cannot say that I was in the least bit comfortable. I lived alone. It's late at night, and I just met this man that is much older than I am. I knew what God wanted me to do, but this went way beyond anything I had ever done before. We left church and stopped to get something to eat. We talked some, which helped me get a little bit more comfortable before I brought this stranger into my one-bedroom apartment.

I couldn't help but seem to wonder things like, "What if this guy is a serial killer?" He wasn't very talkative, which didn't help me get much more comfortable. In one sense, I trust God. Otherwise, I wouldn't be doing this. I know that God wouldn't ask me to do something that will bring me harm, but my mind seemed to be thinking about the worst possible scenarios.

We finish eating and head to my apartment. I show him where he can sleep in the one bedroom, and I explain that I will be staying in the living room. I put a towel and washcloth for him in the bathroom.

I try to settle down for the night in the living room, but my mind is racing. Do I really have some strange man in here that I just met? I was hoping that the man would close the bedroom door for the night. That way, if he tried to get up, I would hear the door open. I remember lying down and being glad that I was close to the main door of the apartment. I felt like I could get out easily if I needed to.

I lay there wide awake. Then, I felt like I didn't even want to go to sleep. I wanted to stay on guard. If I fell asleep, I felt like I would be in an even more vulnerable position. In case this man got any crazy ideas, I didn't want to be asleep.

This was one of the most unusual nights of my life. As I lay there thinking the worst, God spoke to me. He said, "Perfect love casts out all fear." He said this to me several times during that night.

This is in Scripture. If I understood how much God loved me, I wouldn't fear anything in this situation. This was stretching me in the most uncomfortable way.

The night passed by without incident. When morning came, I was faced with another dilemma. I wanted to take a shower before church. Although the bathroom door had a lock on it, I knew it would be easy for someone to get in there if they really wanted to.

What to do, what to do? I remembered what God had said about perfect love casting out all fear, but this was requiring even further trust. I sensed that this wasn't so much about whether or not I trusted this stranger but whether or not I trusted God.

After thinking about it a lot and talking to God, I decided to take the shower. Not only would I take a shower, but as a sheer act of trust, I wouldn't even lock the door. This was probably the fastest shower I've ever taken. Again, nothing happened.

Eventually, I had to knock on the bedroom door to let the man know that we would need to leave for church soon. I

I Found God Outside of Church

brought him to church with me that day and then to the bus station after church. I got him a ticket for the next city he was headed to, and that was that. Honestly, I was kind of relieved to drop him off and get my life back.

I believe that this was a moment of testing. Some of these moments are less enjoyable than others, yet the peace that I have from obeying the One who gave up Jesus for me surpasses any discomfort I've ever gone through.

What is God asking you to do the next time you are passing someone by? What will your answer be?

This wasn't the last test I was given. The next would come when I was very tired.

5
Tired

Have you ever been so tired that you didn't want to talk, think, move, or anything else? That was me one April day in 2012. All I wanted was to complete everything that needed to be done and then go plop on my chair on the beach. It was tax time. 2011 was my first year living in a state that has state income taxes. Actually, I had lived in two states during the year, so I wasn't looking forward to doing my taxes.

I had been very busy and was extremely tired. This was the latest that I had ever waited to do my taxes. I found a website that seemed easy to use and began to input all of my information. This was very time-consuming and mentally exhausting. After I had completed all of my federal tax questions, the software asked me about my state taxes.

As I answered the questions, it asked me if I lived in more than one state during the year. I said yes; now, the site tells me that they can't help me with my state income taxes. Are you kidding me? I've just spent several hours inputting all of my information, and now, you're telling me that you can only help me with half of what I need to do?

I was frustrated, yet, I couldn't stop until this was done. I was out of time and couldn't put this off any longer. I then found another website and began the process all over again. What a relief it was when I finally completed this task! All I could think of was getting to the beach and being able to relax, not think, and not do anything.

I headed to the beach, parked my car, and began walking through the sand with my somewhat heavy chair in hand. I wanted to get away from as much noise as possible. This would require walking some distance. I finally reached a somewhat secluded spot and breathed a sigh of relief as I plopped down into my chair. I could rest at last!

Then, suddenly, Jesus speaks to me. "Come, take a walk with me." I can feel His presence there strongly. In one sense, I'm in awe that Jesus is talking to me and wants to walk with me. On another level though, I'm thinking, "Really, now of all times, when I'm so tired and want to do nothing?" He patiently

I Found God Outside of Church

waited for my answer. I was so tired. This really felt like a hard decision. Deep within me, I knew that I needed to get up. Somehow, I did. I began to walk on the beach with Jesus.

It was immediately exhilarating. Words can't describe how much excitement I felt walking on the beach with Him. I wanted to reach down and grab His hand as we walked. Although I couldn't see Him, His presence was very strong. He seemed tangible.

We walked and walked. He didn't say anything as we walked. I wondered where we were going. I realized that this was further than I had ever walked on the beach before. I had never come this far. We continued to walk, and at some point, He stopped. I wondered why we were stopping. I began to look around since we had stopped right in front of the water around this one corner. As I stood there, more dolphins than I have ever seen in my life appeared. They were jumping and splashing and having a great time. I cannot explain my joy, awe, and excitement. I had never seen anything like this in my life. Up to this point, I hadn't seen any dolphins at the beach.

I stood there completely amazed. I was speechless. At some point, Jesus said to me, "Imagine what else I will show you if you continue to follow me." And then, just as suddenly as He had come, He left.

I stood there frozen. To think that I had almost missed this! To think that I had contemplated sitting in my chair and turning up this! This one sentence impacted me greatly. Jesus took me further than I had ever gone, and He didn't make me go by myself either. Then, what He allowed me to see when I did follow Him was so beautiful. Imagine the things that He has for us if we will only trust Him enough to follow Him.

God's ways are definitely higher than our ways, and His timing is definitely not our timing. I'm so glad that I got up from that spot that day. His plans for my day were far better than any that I could've come up with. I will always cherish this walk on the beach with Jesus.

What will your answer be if Jesus asks something of you when you're very tired?

This wouldn't be the last time that Jesus would use the beach to teach me a lesson.

6
Lost

A friend of mine had come from Tennessee to visit me in Savannah, Georgia. I was honored that she chose to come and see me, as it was her first vacation that she had had by herself since her kids were born. They were now grown. She mainly wanted to go to the beach and to not have to think, plan, or drive – all of the things that she had had to do for years as a single mom.

We had great weather while she was here. It was late spring. We went to the beach, went for a long walk, and just enjoyed the ocean breeze. As we walked along, we were suddenly overtaken by water. The water went from barely touching our feet to almost up to our knees in just a few seconds. I looked up and saw that a large cargo ship was passing by. The ship had pushed all of this water on shore and onto us.

Just as quickly as the water came, it also receded. It happened so fast. Many sea creatures had washed up on the shore. There was a huge, round, brown object floating close by. I had to look closely. I thought that it was a sea turtle; it was so large. As I got closer, I saw that it was a horseshoe crab.

When I surveyed the scene around me, I saw that many small fish had also been washed ashore. The fish were trapped in these small pockets of sand that were separated from the ocean. I immediately realized that if these fish were not put back into the ocean, they would die on the shore.

I went to the first small fish and gently tried to scoop him up. He was very resistant and definitely did not want me to touch him. He started floundering around and flopped his way out of my hands. I was there to save his life, but he didn't seem to think so. I gently scooped him up again and noticed that there was a small stream of water close by that was connected to the ocean. There were still other fish to save, so I put the little fish in the stream facing the ocean and gently pushed him in the direction that he needed to go.

To my dismay, the fish turned around, swam directly back onto the shore, and got stuck again. I said: "Fish, I'm trying to help you." I went back to the same little fish, gently scooped him up again, and again, put him in the stream facing the ocean with a slight nudge in the direction that he needed to go. The stubborn little fish again thought he knew best, again turned his body around, swam back onto the shore, and got stuck again.

I was getting irritated, but I still went to the little fish a third time. He didn't seem quite as resistant as when we first started. Maybe he finally realized that he needed some help. After picking him up and placing him in the stream facing the ocean for the third time, he took off into the right direction. Finally! I was relieved and could now quickly go and save the others.

My friend and I spent a bit more time at the beach and then headed back to my apartment. I decided to get cleaned up before dinner that night. As I was in the shower, God spoke to me, "You were that fish."

The revelation of how I was once struggling for breath, dying on my own, going the wrong direction, needing help, yet resisting the One who was there to save me just like the fish was powerful. That was me before I ended up at the bottom of my closet floor. The realization that I had thought I had known best in my life, particularly in relationships, was also true. Not realizing that God was good and was there to help me and not judge or hurt me was also true. Still struggling with going backwards after He helped me was also true. Some fish I was!

This broke me in a good way. Due to bad church experiences and my own upbringing, I hadn't understood that God was good and that I could trust Him fully. I didn't know that it was safe to trust Him with all of me. It took me being broken and feeling lost and hopeless before I turned to Him with all of me. Like the fish, I had run out of other options. God came to me when I was at my worst, and He loved me! He never gave up on me, even after I tried turning back to my old ways several times. He continued to help me and save me from myself no matter how many times I resisted Him. He continues to help me each day that I turn to Him.

The Lord is ready to rescue whoever is lost. And it may happen in just a few seconds!

God continued to help me understand who He is and who I am, but would He give me answers regarding other people in my life that didn't seem to want anything to do with Him?

7
Running

It was a beautiful, sunny day in Tampa, Florida. I was visiting a friend who was scheduled to be baptized that weekend. We went to the beach in the Clearwater area the day before her baptism was scheduled. We had great weather around 80 degrees.

Although it was a gorgeous day, I was a bit distracted. I had another friend that I will refer to as Brad that I was concerned about. Brad's behavior was erratic, and he didn't seem to know what he wanted or where he was going in life. I didn't really understand what was going on with him, but I really cared and wanted to understand. I decided to go for a walk on the beach to clear my head and ask God for some answers. I was struggling to hear from the Lord regarding Brad.

I felt led to walk and walk. I'm not sure how far I went, but it was very far. I felt frustrated while I was walking. The wind was blowing from behind me, and it was blowing my hair into my face and into my eyes. I kept having to move it out of my face. I started to wonder where I was going and what the point was. I continued to seek God, but I just felt led to keep walking. It felt like I had gone several miles. I walked until I couldn't walk anymore. Eventually, I plopped down on the sand and just sat.

I didn't understand at all what the point of the walk was. I was still waiting for the Lord to speak to me. Eventually, I got up and decided that it was time to turn around and go back the other way. I knew that my friend was way down there and that I should start heading back towards her.

As I began to return in the direction I had come from, I was overwhelmed. It was so beautiful. Now, the wind was blowing in my face, keeping my hair away from my eyes. Also, the sun was shining on the water, and the reflection was gorgeous! I hadn't experienced any of this when I was headed the other way. I was overwhelmed by the beauty of what I was experiencing.

What a difference it made to turn around and go the other way. As I continued to walk, the Lord began to speak to me. He explained that this was exactly what Brad was going through. He was headed in the wrong direction. He said that eventually, Brad would get tired of going the direction he was going.

I Found God Outside of Church

Eventually, he would turn around. He said that Brad had no idea what he was missing right now.

God is so amazing. He knows all of the answers to everything. And I do mean everything! He loves to speak to us in unique ways that are easy for us to understand. And He uses whatever is around us and His creation to reveal things to us. I just love Him!

The following week when I spoke to Brad, he told me that he had been "running." I understood that to mean that he had been running from God and from God's will for his life. I told him of my experience on the beach, and he said that that described exactly what had been going on in his life.

Who do you know that is headed in the wrong direction? Is it you? Have you been headed that direction for long? Are you asking what the point is? Are you ready to turn around? If so, just say yes to Jesus today. He longs to embrace you.

Is it a family member, friend, child, coworker, or neighbor that's going in the wrong direction? Be encouraged that eventually, he or she will start to ask what the point is and will get tired of going that direction. Eventually, they will turn around! Believe it today!

Although I loved all of the times that God spoke to me on the beach, one of the next places He chose to speak to me took me by surprise. And what He would ask me to do would take me further out of my comfort zone than anything else ever had.

8

Brazil

Have you experienced a day that significantly changed your life? Sunday, June 1, 2014, was that day for me. Church had just dismissed. In the parking lot, I ran into a woman named Lisa that was around my age. I knew she was going on a mission trip, although I didn't know where. We began to make small talk, and out of nowhere, I blurted out, "If there's ever a last-minute opening on the trip, let me know, and I'll pray about going."

She immediately said, "There's an opening now." Uh oh. "What am I getting myself into?" I thought to myself. She gave me a few details, and I told her that I would pray about it and let her know. I didn't even know what country she was going to. I wasn't looking to go on a mission trip. There are plenty of people that need help locally. I know some people who feel called to missions abroad, but I had never heard that call.

I got in my car and had a somewhat uneasy feeling. I immediately started talking to God and told Him, "If this is something that You want me to do, I need for You to show me clearly." That was it. There was no long prayer, and I was straight to the point.

I had some time before I met a friend for lunch and realized that I was in the same area as a cemetery where a dear friend of mine had recently been buried. I hadn't been by there since the day of the funeral. Monice was such a gem. I know that God put her in my life. She was one of the kindest and most encouraging people I have ever met. We connected at my old church right away. She was in her eighties, but that didn't matter. We became good friends almost immediately. She was so easy to talk to, gentle, understanding, and sympathetic. I took her on Saturdays to get her hair done, and then, we would go to McDonald's. I don't really care for McDonald's very much, but it always tasted so good and was so enjoyable when she and I went. Those days were such blessings.

I headed to the cemetery and wondered if I would even remember where she was buried. It was an unusually beautiful day outside. The sun was out, there was a slight breeze, and it

I Found God Outside of Church

wasn't too hot or too cold. As I got to the cemetery, various statues caught my eye. For some reason, I like to look at statues of Jesus. I like to see if they resonate with me as reflecting His character or not. I went to where I believed Monice was buried, parked my car, and began to walk around. I had total peace. It wasn't a sad time for me at all. I know she's in a better place; she was a Christian.

It seems strange to have so much peace wandering around a cemetery, but that's exactly how I felt. Far in the distance, I could see a statue of what looked like a book. I couldn't help but notice it and be drawn to it. Something seemed to be pulling me in that direction. I tried to push it aside because I wanted to look at the other statues, particularly any that were of Jesus. I looked around at some of the statues, but I knew that I must go and see the book.

I made my way over to the marble-looking statue of an open book. When I read the first word, I froze. The power of that one word hit me over the head, rushed through my entire being, and left me speechless. "Go." I stood frozen because I knew that God was speaking to me. The power in this one word was so intense. Somewhere deep within me, I knew that I was looking at the answer to my question. But I didn't know if I was ready for this answer.

I stood there, and all I could hear was, "Go." I said, "Ok, Lord, I want to make sure that this is You speaking to me." I looked down, and two headstones from where I was standing, I saw my first name. I'm hearing and seeing the answer to my question. I'm somewhat amazed and in awe, but still, I say, "Ok Lord, I still want to make sure that this is You speaking to me." In case what was already happening wasn't clear enough, I went on to read the rest of the saying on the book in front of me. It was a quote from the Bible that says: "Go ye therefore and teach all nations, baptizing them in the name of the Father, and of the Son, and of the Holy Ghost: teaching them to observe all things whatsoever I have commanded you. And lo, I am with you alway even unto the end of the world. Amen."

I was somewhat incredulous at what was happening. I had a sense that I was way out of any kind of familiar elements. I knew from previous experience that it's very important to act right away when God speaks. If I wait, I know that the power and urgency of the prompting will diminish. Also, if I wait, I know that I or the devil may try to talk me out of what I've been told. So, as soon as I got to my car, I knew that I needed to act right away and be obedient to what God had just spoken to me. I texted the woman from church and told her that I know that God wants me to go. I asked her to put me in contact with the right person. I wanted to make myself accountable to what I had just been told.

I literally got the answer not only on the same day but within an hour of asking God that question. "And you will seek Me and find Me, when you search for Me with all your heart" (Jeremiah 29:13, NKJV).

There were many details to act on quickly in order to travel out of the country. I had an old passport that needed to be updated, and I also would need a visa for this trip, which was only two months away. Nothing is too hard for God, but the time crunch for the passport and visa were felt.

There were only two post offices in the area that helped with passports. Both required that you make an appointment. After calling both, I got an appointment for a few days later. When I arrived, the woman told me that they don't make appointments for the quarter-of-the-hour time slots. She looked in the book and saw that someone "made a mistake" and put me in there for the quarter of the hour. She said that they usually only make appointments for every half hour. Otherwise, she said that there was a one-month wait for the next appointment. She accepted my paperwork, took my picture, and sent it off for my new passport. Look at God! If God wants something done, He will make a way! They thought it was a mistake, but I knew that it was the favor of God.

Once the passport arrived in the mail several weeks later, I then made an appointment in Atlanta, Georgia, to get the visa. The appointment went smoothly, but you don't receive your visa on the spot. They process it and mail it to you. We were leaving the following week for Brazil. I had to trust that God would get it to me in time. I did receive it days before I was to board the plane. In the past, I always liked to plan way ahead. I would've preferred that everything was done far in advance, but where would the faith have been in that? The decision to go on this trip was already stretching my faith greatly.

I Found God Outside of Church

In the time leading up to the trip, I sensed that this was going to be unlike anything I had experienced up to this point in my life. I really had no idea what I was in for.

We left on August 13, 2014. There were 19 of us on the trip. The first area we went to was Rio de Janeiro. A local church where we were going to minister had offered to house and feed us. We didn't know the specifics until we got there, but we were told to bring bed sheets. Seventeen of us stayed in a two-bedroom house with one bathroom. The crazy thing was that this was actually very doable. I never would've guessed that we could all function well in such close quarters.

There was usually a line for the bathroom. You might be asked, "On a scale of 1-10, how badly do you need to go?" Depending on your answer, you might get to go to the front of the line. Some showered in the morning, and some showered at night. I found that the best time to shower was at lunch. When everyone else was eating, I could have the bathroom to myself and not feel rushed.

I really enjoyed this part of the trip. We all bonded really well in this close living environment. The lack of physical space and privacy forced us to communicate more, and it tore down walls between us. There were 3 beds in the house. The rest of us had 1-2" thick, twin-size mats to sleep on on the concrete floor. It was definitely humbling, yet I felt grateful for what they offered us. The family that lived in this 2-bedroom house had moved out of their home for us to be able to use it for those few days. They felt that it was an honor to be able to do this for us.

Each morning when I woke up, there was this sweet lady named Jane in the kitchen cooking for us. She was always smiling. She seemed to really enjoy doing this for us. It seemed like she was in the kitchen morning, noon, and night standing over the hot stove preparing food for us. I will always remember her smile. She really blessed me.

We were told by our leader that before we arrived, the church didn't have the funds to feed us. They had mentioned to their church that we were coming and had explained that there was a financial need in order to feed us. Feeding almost twenty adults three meals a day for 4-5 days wasn't cheap. The cost of food was expensive in Brazil. The wages were also much lower there. Many families in Brazil didn't own a vehicle. Some owned a small motorcycle, similar to a moped. We were told about a man who heard about the need. He only had one means of transportation – his motorcycle. He gave his motorcycle to the church in order for them to sell it to be able to feed us.

I was greatly impacted when I heard this. It almost hurt to receive such a costly gift. I had never known this type of sacrificial giving in America. We seem to have so much more regarding material things, yet I had never heard of anything close to this gift. I never got to meet this man, yet he greatly touched my life. I will never forget his sacrifice.

The church where we were ministering had outgrown their space and needed a larger facility. They were having trouble getting a property that would fit their needs and was still in the same area. There was a specific property that they were interested in, and one of the pastors took several of us there. When we got there, we laid our hands on the wall surrounding the building as we began to pray. It was a beautiful day. The sun was shining brightly upon us. I heard one woman next to me thanking God for giving this property to the church. She prayed as though it was already done. This was a teachable moment for me. I wasn't used to praying this way.

We found out later that day that there were people working inside this building when we were there. They said that they felt something like an earthquake inside the building when we were there praying. Around that time, the owner of the property called his son who was inside the building. The owner was driving over a nearby bridge and had caught a glimpse of several Americans outside his building. When the father talked to the son and heard about the shaking of the building, he said that he knew God wanted him to give this building to the church. He agreed that very day to do just that. Interestingly, we couldn't feel this earthquake-type sensation outside where we were.

That night, we went to the property that would become the church's new location. The owner met us there to let us in. We prayed over the building and praised and worshipped God. It was a joyous occasion.

Our last night in this city was also a very memorable one. My friend Lisa wanted to do something for the people who had hosted us. The pastors of the church and those who had served us by cooking, giving up their home, and being our security were

I Found God Outside of Church

there. They had thrown a farewell party for us. Lisa wanted to do something special for them. Getting flowers for the women was suggested, but they would die quickly. Plus, what would we get for the men? Lisa decided that she wanted to wash their feet. I had never had my feet washed or seen anyone else's feet washed. I didn't know what to expect.

What I got to witness that night was one of the most moving spiritual experiences. The tears and weeping that came from those who sat in that circle and had their feet washed was something that I will never forget. I stood in awe that I got to see such an intimate moment that these beautiful, Brazilian brothers and sisters-in-Christ experienced. I later wondered why I had never experienced such a thing in the U.S. This was something that I wanted to bring back with me. I hoped that I would get to bless others this way in the future.

There were so many miracles that we got to witness and take part in. It seemed that God had lined up many things for us. The main things that we had to do were simply say yes and show up. We got to be a part of many incredible things. These two weeks in Brazil were so rich and so full. I felt like I received ten years' worth of spiritual blessings packed into two weeks.

All of this did come at a cost. The cost to go out of the country for two weeks wasn't cheap. There was also the time off work. For some, this was all the vacation time they had for the entire year, yet they used it to go on this trip. Also, there was definite discomfort going into many unknowns in a new area.

I've learned that the blessings of obedience to God always far outweigh the cost. If there's great cost involved in obeying the Lord and following Him, how much greater will the blessings be?

When we got on the plane to leave that first area of Brazil, I cried. That place and those people had impacted me so much.

Going to Brazil wouldn't be the last time that God would get me out of my comfort zone. Now, He would ask me to go on an adventure in my own country.

9
Adventure

In 2016, I reconnected with a guy that I had known in my childhood. We had liked each other in elementary school but had gone our separate ways in high school. He was now living in New York and invited me to visit. He told me that many other people from the area where we grew up had come and visited. He wanted to show me around the city and began telling me about the things he wanted me to see. He offered that I could stay at his place, and he would stay with his folks.

I love to travel, so it wasn't a hard decision to choose to go on this trip. Of course, I wondered what might grow between us after reconnecting in person.

We began talking every day. He even mentioned that he had looked up jobs like mine in his area. It seemed that we both wondered what could become of our friendship.

Meanwhile, I had something happen that I hadn't experienced before. I had a dream about a homeless man in New York. I saw myself praying for him and him being healed. It seemed that some things were building before this trip.

Shortly before the trip, the guy tells me that he's had a change of heart and doesn't think he can continue in something that feels like too much work in the beginning. I said that that was fine, but what about the trip?

He said that he didn't see the point in me coming now. I saw the point. I already had a ticket, and all arrangements had already been made. I knew that he had family in the area, and it was only a weekend visit, not a marriage proposal.

I began to pray about whether or not I should go. God put on my heart to still go on the trip.

In the past, I've run from rejection. At the slightest hint of rejection, I would remove myself from a situation before the other person could. Now, God is leading me to travel from Georgia to New York and on some level, face rejection. Hmm.

I told the guy that I still planned to come. I packed and readied for a trip with many unknowns. I assumed that the guy would at minimum pick me up from the airport and set me up to stay with one of his family members.

I Found God Outside of Church

Unfortunately, I was wrong. Although he had initiated this, he left me stranded at the airport upon arrival. He said that he was busy and surely, I had a credit card for a hotel.

I asked God what to do, and God told me that I should still stay in New York for those few days. I didn't want to be put out any more than I already had, so I wasn't going to get a hotel. I ended up staying at the airport.

Thankfully, JFK airport in New York is a busy airport with many international flights. It's not uncommon to have people sleeping in the airport as they wait for their connecting flight or a delayed flight.

I wondered why I was there and why this was happening.

At least two important things happened. First, God had me press in further as far as facing and standing up to rejection. God put on my heart to go see the guy who didn't seem to want me there. This was more than uncomfortable. Like I said, I've run from the slightest hint of rejection in the past.

God led me to go to his job, where he was a manager. He had called me many times from his work, so I was able to call that number and get an address.

After arriving and telling the receptionist my name and that I was a personal friend, I waited. I didn't know if he would actually see me. It was nerve-racking and had taken quite a few steps for me to find the place through public transportation and while toting my small suitcase on wheels.

Uncomfortable isn't a strong enough word to describe how I felt waiting in the reception area. I had bought some things for his son prior to the trip and wanted to drop them off. I also wanted to be obedient to what the Lord was telling me to do.

Surprisingly, I was invited back to his office. It was strange and awkward seeing him after all of those years and after what had happened the night before.

I told him that it was good to see him and that I wouldn't take up much of his time. I gave him the items for his son, which he said he didn't feel comfortable receiving. I told him that I didn't have anything else to do with the items, and I insisted on leaving them there. He seemed busy, and after a couple of minutes of small talk, he offered to walk me out.

I left the office and ended up on a nearby beach. I talked to God some and cried. It wasn't easy facing this person from my past. It wasn't easy to run to rejection and not away from it. But my worth doesn't come from this guy or what he thinks about me. My worth comes from God alone.

After that, I headed back to the airport. Attempting to sleep and get cleaned up at the airport for those few days wasn't easy, but it was doable. At least I had some shelter and access to toilets and water.

The next day, I was determined to get out and enjoy the day. I wanted to go on top of the Rockefeller Center building and also explore Manhattan. I enjoy being able to look out over a city. I got to Manhattan and began to explore the area near Times Square. It was busy and somewhat congested, but I managed to get around with my suitcase on wheels.

As I was looking for Rockefeller Center, I saw in the distance a man that appeared to be homeless. As I got closer, I realized that he was the man in my dream! As I approached him, I was overwhelmed with compassion for him. I could feel God's love for him. The experience was somewhat surreal. This was the second important thing that happened on this trip.

I stopped and said hello. He looked to be in his early 50's and had a thick, Spanish accent. He seemed physically fit and had dark brown hair, medium brown skin, and brown eyes. I sat next to him on the bench, and we talked about life, work, God, and other things. He had a phone from his sister that he didn't know how to use very well, so I helped him with it. His thick, Spanish accent, along with his phone language being set to Spanish, caused this to take a while. I was in no hurry though.

I discovered that he only had one contact in his phone – his sister. This broke my heart. I couldn't imagine only having one human contact in the world.

I noticed people staring at us as they would pass by. One man came close and hung around trying to figure out what we were talking about. I ended up staying with the homeless man for a few hours. It was a strange feeling to be sitting next to the man that I had seen in my dream a couple of weeks before that. It was a very powerful experience.

I invited him to come with me to Rockefeller Center, but he said that they wouldn't let him in. I assumed that he was self-conscious about his appearance and that maybe he had been treated cruelly in the past. I tried to convince him to come with

I Found God Outside of Church

me, but he declined. I gave him an envelope from my purse that had all the cash I had with me, but I felt like it wasn't enough. The love of God for this man was so vast. I could feel it. I didn't feel that there was enough I could do to express God's love to this man.

Eventually, I felt that it was time to go. I asked him if I could pray for him before I left. It was weird though because I sensed that the man was already healed during our time together.

After praying for him, I put my phone number into his phone. Now, he would have two contacts in the world. He wanted to write my number down on something else too in case he ever got separated from his phone. It's difficult to explain the experience, but it was the most powerful time on my trip.

I then went to Rockefeller Center. It was interesting to see how much more of the city I could see from a higher position. I sensed God speaking that the view from above is so much different than the view from below.

I spent my last night at the airport and got up the next day to go to church. I traveled by train to a church where I heard a powerful message about the time when the people were stoning Stephen in the Bible. The pastor related that the people were rejecting the God inside of Stephen more than they were rejecting Stephen.

After this, I was ready to go home. I was exhausted and not sad in the least bit to leave New York. I was glad that I went, even though it was nothing like I could've imagined. I came out of that weekend much stronger than before.

There is a time to face things. What or whom are you being called to face? Will you be obedient? What powerful experiences will God have for you as you are obedient?

Although a lot of my experiences with God have been outside of church, I've also had some great things happen at church.

10
Other Church Experiences

Have you ever made any friends at church or had anything else good happen to you at church? I've met some amazing people at church over the years.

There was a wonderful couple in the church that I grew up in that was like family to me. They would have me over to spend the night, would play games with me, and would take me to the grocery store and let me pick out any item that I wanted. They would also take me out to eat. These were huge things that I didn't get to do with my own family.

My family was poor, and our home was a very volatile environment. This couple's home was like a safe haven. They truly loved me. I played lots of games with the husband. While we were playing, the wife would offer me a red, delicious apple. She would peel it, cut it up, and bring it in a bowl to me. It tasted better than candy. I would eat the whole thing. Then she would ask me if I wanted another one. I would say yes. After I finished the second one, she offered me another. She did that three times in a row for me. I've never eaten any apples that tasted as good since then. I now know that it was the love behind them that made them taste so good.

Another amazing person from the church that I grew up in was the pastor of that church. This man was a true shepherd. He genuinely loved God and people. When things would get bad in our home between my parents, sometimes, my mother, my sisters, and I would go to someone else's house until things cooled down. We stayed at my pastor's house a couple of times.

He also made a special effort when someone graduated from high school or there was some other special occasion to take them out to eat. I remember one time when he ate at the restaurant that I was working in as a teenager. He came up and gave me a wonderful hug. It was the kind that makes you know that the person really loves you and is genuinely glad to see you.

This pastor recognized a gift in me. In my early teen years, we had a teen newspaper in our church. Many people in the youth group were involved. I wrote a couple of articles here and

I Found God Outside of Church

there. The pastor sought me out at church one day and gave me two books from his personal library. Both were regarding how to write your first book. I didn't know what to think or what to do with those books. I definitely didn't see myself as a writer at the time or think that it would be a profession for me. I set them aside, but I kept them for many years through various moves, including a move to another state. Although I may have had some bad experiences in the church, this man of God recognized a gift and calling on my life at an early age. Over two decades later, here I am writing my first book.

I've found that church is a place of connection. I've had important connections made in the church. Many other great relationships of mine have also begun in the church.

I once was at a church that I hadn't been attending for long when I was in my 20's. I was in a class on Sunday mornings at this church. I didn't feel like many people had reached out to me or had made me feel very welcome. God spoke to me and said, "When someone new comes, they're probably thinking that same thing about you." Basically, people didn't know that I wasn't a member and other things that I was expecting them to know. Also, if I saw a problem, I needed to be part of the solution, rather than perpetuating the problem. God told me to watch the door for the next person that came in the class and to make a point to go to them and make them feel welcome, so I did.

I was still pretty shy at the time, so this was way out of my comfort zone. The next person that walked through the door was a woman. I sat by her, and we started talking. We ended up going to lunch together after church. In a short time, she became the best friend that I had ever had. I could talk to her about anything. We related to each other really well. She was truly an angel to me in the darkest season of my life when I was still living in Tennessee. She was there for me, supported me, and loved me without judging me for the decisions that I had made. If I hadn't put forth effort to befriend her, we may have never become friends. "A man who has friends must himself be friendly" (Proverbs 18:24, NKJV). If you want a friend, be a friend.

When I moved to Savannah in 2011, I met an amazing woman at church that I eventually called my adopted mother.

Other Church Experiences

She was like the mom I never had – very encouraging, affirming, and supportive. I would call her on my way home from work. She was always interested in what was going on in my life and was always so positive. She was hilarious too. We had a great time together.

I also met at church the person who would tell me about the trip to Brazil. That was truly a life-changing trip for me. I grew so much during those two weeks. I would've missed out on that opportunity if I hadn't been at the right church at the right time. She later became a great friend of mine.

Another friend who was really there for me and was so supportive leading up to my time of leaving for Brazil was also a friend from church. He prayed and fasted for me while I was gone and also picked me up from the airport when I got back.

Some of my positive church experiences have also come from serving in the church. I've found much joy and purpose in my life through serving in the church. I once visited a church that had no pastor and no class for my age group. I thought to myself, "What can this church do for me?" The Lord spoke to me that day and said, "It's not, what can this church do for you. It's, what can you do for this church?" That perspective changes a lot of things.

I've found much more joy when I was giving of myself at church rather than when I simply received whatever everyone else had prepared. It really is more blessed to give than to receive. I've had people come to me and say that the lesson that I taught in Sunday school spoke right to their current situation. I've also had the privilege of praying with people and leading them in a prayer of salvation and a new life with God.

I've also gotten freed of some of my own insecurities through serving in the church. There have been times that God has asked me to do the last thing in the world that I would have ever seen myself doing. For example, I have no musical background of any kind. I knew nothing about music. When my music teacher in junior high school told us that he was going to have us sing the scale for him by ourselves, I was intentionally absent that day.

At some point as an adult, God asked me to join the worship team at church. What? Are you serious? It was hard enough for me to teach in front of a Sunday school class. Teaching for the

I Found God Outside of Church

first time was a big stretch for me. Now, You want me to stand on a stage, hold a microphone, and sing in front of the church? Umm, yes, that's exactly what God asked me to do.

He's worth it, and I didn't want to disobey or hold up my own growth, so I reluctantly said yes. Even though this was a small church, this was very uncomfortable for me. I would hold the microphone down closer to my stomach rather than my mouth because I didn't want anyone to hear me. As far as parts go, I have no idea what part I was singing – probably different parts at different times.

They used to ask me to hold the microphone closer to my mouth, but I tried to avoid that. The truth is that God wants to free us of insecurities and grow us, which usually involves discomfort. If you have a fear or an insecurity in any area, the best way to overcome it is to face it head-on.

One friend of mine had a huge fear of needles. As God grew him, he felt led to give blood and intentionally face his fear of needles, so he did. I was very impressed and proud of him for doing that.

God also wanted me to know that being on the worship team was less about the singing and the sound of my voice as it was about worshipping Him in spirit and in truth. Singing for Him and to Him from a place of gratitude for what He had done in my life was the most important thing. Worship should never be about us, yet it was hard not to think about myself when I was holding a microphone with literal spotlights on me and with people in the audience looking at me.

Three years later, I was on a mission trip to Brazil, and someone from the local church's worship team came to me and asked if I would pray with the worship team and talk to them. Me? Out of our entire group, they're singling me out to pray for them? Joining the worship team back home hadn't only been about freeing me of insecurities or worshipping God. God also wanted to use me to bless others in this area and share with them what I had learned along the way about worship.

Later, in another church, God yet again asked me to join the worship team. This was a much larger church than the first one. God was indirect with me this time. He prompted me to talk to the worship leader after service one evening. I enjoy encouraging others. I wasn't really sure what we would talk

Other Church Experiences

about, but I figured that God just wanted me to encourage the worship leader. When I went to him, the first thing that popped out of his mouth was, "When are you going to join us?" Uh oh, here we go again. I said yes and joined shortly thereafter. It was an experience.

Whether teaching, being part of a worship team, or serving in any other area of church, I've found it very rewarding. Getting to pour back out to others what God has done in my life and impact people's lives for eternity are amazing things. All of us have gifts that God has put inside of us. Sometimes, we don't know what they are, but we know that there's a need in the church, and we know that we can help fill that need. So, fill it, and be a blessing.

God will allow a certain amount of spiritual attacks to come at you. He knows what you can handle with His help. As I mentioned earlier, when you face opposition or resistance, yet push through and don't give up, you come out much stronger. I call it "growing pains." It's often painful to grow, yet God loves you too much to see you stay where you are spiritually.

Even though I had thought that guy was my friend that came at me right before I taught Sunday school for the first time, good things came out of that attack. First, I searched the Scriptures even further on the subject of women speaking in a co-ed setting. I knew what the Lord had told me to do, but I sought the Lord again, and He led me to Scripture that confirmed what I already knew. I found several things, but the thing that stood out the most to me was that when Jesus rose from the dead, the first people that He appeared to and revealed Himself to, were women. Not only did He appear to these women, but He basically told them to go tell the disciples (many men) what they had seen. This was not an accident or a coincidence. God reveals Himself to both men and women, and He can and does use either to be a blessing to the other.

Secondly, once I realized that this was an attack from Satan, I had even more resolve to do what God had called me to do. Often times, you will know that an attack is from Satan by the pain that comes with the attack. That guy's words and tone were very mean, harsh, and cutting. I had an extra strength and determination when I went to teach the class after the attempt to get me to back down. As strange as it may sound,

I Found God Outside of Church

I'm thankful that this happened. I put this incident into my positive church experiences because I gained a lot from the experience. Again, sometimes the good and the bad are part of the same thing.

I've also grown a lot spiritually by going to church. I inadvertently learned the most about Satan and how he works through people by going to church. I learned so much when I was under a lot of spiritual attack while serving in different churches. This is how I learned about spiritual warfare and how the devil likes to work through people in churches, especially through people on the church staff.

I've also had my perspective changed in many ways that it needed to be. I've already shared many of those changes with you. On the last worship team that I was on, I used to pray when we came out on the stage, "Lord, help them to see You and not us." God grew me from a place where I was initially focused on me to a place where I realized that worship is all about Him. I found myself closing my eyes a lot so that I could focus on the Lord during the songs. Worship should be personal between each person and God. It should never be about the people leading the music.

I'm honestly thankful for each and every spiritual attack because they were all opportunities for me to learn, stand my ground, be tested, and ultimately come out stronger. God knows what we can handle. It was also interesting to see whom the attacks came through. Basically, I knew whom to be praying for and also whom to be on guard around after an attack came through them. I found that often, the attacks came through people who were respected in the church.

One fact that I must mention regarding church is that it represents Jesus' body. 1 Corinthians 12:27 (NIV) says, "Now you are the body of Christ, and each one of you is a part of it." Each part of the body has an important role. The hands, feet, head, back, etc., are all necessary, and all work together to accomplish things.

What part of the church are you? How will the rest of the body be negatively affected if you're not there doing your part? Jesus died for the church. If His body, the church, is broken, and a lot of churches are, will you choose to be part of the solution, rather than the problem? If you sit at home, how will that help

Other Church Experiences

people who need to know who Jesus really is?

It's time for true believers to rise up (sometimes off their couches) and take back what is theirs. It's time to start kicking Satan out of churches. He needs to be afraid when he sees us coming. We need to shine the light of Jesus everywhere we go, especially in the church. That's where many people are looking for Him. Let's tell others what Jesus has done for us. Let's help the one that is in need or hurting. Let's choose to forgive because God forgave us. Let's choose to not run from church when Satan tries to come at us, hurt us, or reject us through the church. The world needs to see true Christians. It's time for us to rise up and take our rightful places.

There are good things waiting for you at church. What are you waiting for?

Whether in church or outside of church, God has taught me many other things that I believe will help you too.

Timing

I battled for some time. Somehow, God helped me to see that that would only make things worse. The circle or cycle of pain and sin wouldn't have ended there. Chance would've then lashed out at me, and the cycle would have only continued. Only by the grace of God and me going to God each day and using all of the spiritual tools and weapons that were available to me, was I able to not continue the cycle of pain and destruction.

There was one important thing though that I had to do if I wanted to be able to truly move forward in my life. If I didn't, I would prevent my own breakthrough.

12
Obstacle to Breakthrough

I've learned that there's one important matter of the heart that can prevent breakthrough: unforgiveness. Who has hurt you the most in your life? The choice to forgive or not to forgive can have long-lasting effects. I'll share a few personal examples of people I've had to forgive in order to be able to move forward in my life.

In chapter 1, I shared with you about my broken heart. I felt deceived, abandoned, and like I had been thrown away. I wasn't able to see at the time that I was also guilty in that situation. It was easy to blame him and the way he handled everything when he changed his mind. How could he not even tell me? He had talked of spending his life with me. It was easy to blame him and to want to make him feel badly for the way he had handled things.

After I moved to Georgia, God helped me to see that I wasn't innocent and also that I needed to truly forgive the man that had hurt me. God worked in my heart and had me praying for Chance and his wife. It wasn't easy, but God even helped me to pray for blessings on their marriage.

Forgiveness is a choice. I could have stayed bitter for the rest of my life if I wanted to. Do you think that would've hurt Chance and his wife? No, it would've hurt me, my life, and those around me.

Unforgiveness can have long-lasting effects and can prevent you from having breakthrough in your life. When I was in Brazil, I had the opportunity to pray for many people. They would come up to the front after the service to receive prayer. People would line up and wait a long time to have someone pray for them. Many people were having physical problems in their bodies and wanted prayer for healing. Anytime anyone wanted prayer, I first listened to them through the translator, but then, I listened for God to direct me in how to minister to each person.

One of the frequent questions that God would have me ask the person in front of me that had a health problem was: "Is there anyone that you need to forgive?" This happened multiple times. A person came forward with an outward issue, and God

I Found God Outside of Church

would reveal that it was a manifestation of an inner issue of the heart. Spiritual conditions affect a person's health. "Beloved, I pray that you may prosper in all things and be in health, just as your soul prospers" (III John 1:2, NKJV). Here, we see that there's a correlation between what's happening in our souls and what's happening in our bodies. If a person's soul isn't healthy, their body won't be either.

Once, I was about to take communion at my church. I asked God to purify my heart and reveal to me if there was anything in me that offended Him or needed to be changed. He said to me that I needed to forgive an ex-boyfriend. "What?" I thought I had. That relationship had ended more than 10 years ago. I thought I had forgiven him. I wasn't thinking about him or about anything he had done wrong anymore. This took me by surprise. I thought that was old news. I thought I had forgiven him.

Sometimes, forgiveness requires more than just words. Sometimes, it requires action.

Not long after that, I was traveling to Memphis, Tennessee, to take care of some business. I would be there for less than 48 hours and needed to get a lot done while there. The first morning I arrived, my friend that I stayed with prayed for me before I headed out. She prayed that the day would look like what God wanted it to look like. When she prayed, this ex-boyfriend came to mind. God began to tell me that I needed to contact him as part of forgiving him.

God said that I should meet with him face to face and ask him to forgive me. I asked God, "What did I do?" It's easier to see where someone else was wrong; it's not as easy to see your own part in things. The Word of God says, "There is none righteous, no, not one" (Romans 3:10, NKJV).

Contacting my ex-boyfriend and asking him to forgive me was the last thing in the world that I wanted to do while I was in town. Yet, I knew that I wouldn't have peace if I ignored this. So, just like that, his phone number came back to me after all those years.

I texted him saying that I was going to be in town until the next day. I asked if he had time to meet with me. I thought to myself that it would not hurt my feelings if he didn't respond.

Apparently, he still had the same phone number because almost immediately, my phone began to ring. It was my ex-boyfriend. I answered and asked if he had time to meet with me. He asked if everything was ok. I said yes, and we agreed to meet that evening at a coffee shop.

I cannot explain how uncomfortable it was going to meet him that night. I had asked God what I was supposed to say. God said to simply tell him that I was sorry for anything that I had said or done that had hurt him.

I arrived before he did. The place was almost empty. I was glad that we would have some privacy. He walked in a few minutes later, came and sat down, and asked me what this was all about. It was strange seeing him after all of those years. I don't usually struggle for words, but I couldn't seem to find the words for what I wanted to say.

I didn't know where to begin. I was a completely different person than when he knew me. How do I explain this journey and why I've contacted him after all of this time?

I asked him to give me a minute and said that I would explain once my drink came out. In the meantime, he said, "In case I never get the chance to say this to you, I'm sorry for anything that I said or did that hurt you."

I sat there dumbstruck. These were words that I had wanted to hear from him years ago. Also, these were the very words that God wanted me to say to him. I expressed the same to him, and we briefly caught up on some other family members. Then, the place was closing, so we left. And that was that.

It was a strange evening – one that I wouldn't have come up with on my own. Sometimes, there's an action that goes along with forgiveness.

There was another time that God revealed to me someone from my past that I needed to forgive. This was from my childhood. It was more than 20 years ago that it had happened. I had forgotten all about it, but God knew what things in my past needed to be dealt with.

When I was around 10 years old, I was at this girl's house. We went to an in-ground swimming pool in their neighborhood. I didn't know how to swim. This girl's dad knew that I couldn't swim. He must've told me that he was going to throw me in, because I remember begging him not to and trying to squirm out of his grasp.

He threw me in anyways. I don't remember too much of

I Found God Outside of Church

what happened next. I guess someone must have pulled me out. I remember coughing and spitting up water.

I don't remember being in contact with them since that time, and I had forgotten all about that incident. But God brought it back to mind more than 20 years later. It amazes me how God knows us better than we know ourselves. He knows what on the inside of us needs to come out. In this instance, God didn't have me track down that man to tell him that I forgave him. It was just a conscious decision.

I've found that often, the first people that need to be forgiven is one's parents. It's rare to find someone who wasn't hurt over the years by their parents or others who raised them.

Many people are familiar with "The Lord's Prayer." It was a prayer that Jesus prayed in Scripture to God the Father. After it's mentioned, it says, "For if you forgive men their trespasses, your heavenly Father will also forgive you. But if you do not forgive men their trespasses, neither will your Father forgive your trespasses" (Matthew 6:14-15, NKJV). How can we be right with God if we don't forgive those who hurt or offend us?

The thing about forgiveness is that it's not a matter of who is right or wrong. Clearly, if the other person hadn't done anything wrong, then there wouldn't be any reason to forgive them. Forgiveness frees you. Forgiveness is about having a clear conscience with God and also about not opening a door in one's life for the enemy, Satan, to come in and do damage. When we choose not to forgive (or anything else that goes against Scripture), we're making ourselves vulnerable for Satan to have a place in our lives.

I cannot imagine being able to forgive others if I hadn't first experienced God's forgiveness of my own sins. Forgiveness is a call of a Christian that should never be ignored. If God has forgiven you for what you've done wrong, who are you to not forgive someone who has wronged you? Jesus paid the price for everyone's sins. One sign of spiritual maturity is how quickly one can forgive another.

And it's time for you to forgive yourself.

If you're looking for breakthrough in your life, forgiveness of those who have hurt you isn't optional. Who has hurt you the most? Whom is God calling you to forgive? Is it yourself? What action is God calling you to take today as an act of obedience?

Obstacle to Breakthrough

Breakthrough awaits you on the other side of forgiveness.

Once I forgave Chance for his part in things, God gave me several tools to help me overcome the pain and hopelessness that I was feeling. These tools can also help you overcome anything that you're facing.

13
Tools for Overcoming

Are you an overcomer? I believe that you are! I believe that you've already overcome much, and God is going to continue to help you overcome anything you're facing now and anything that may come your way in the future.

With the help of God, I went from being a shy, insecure girl who always wanted to be in the back of a room to now speaking in front of groups of people. Instead of sitting at home with no real purpose or adventure in my life, I've traveled abroad and have gotten to do and see many amazing things. I'll share some of those adventures later in this book.

I shared how God healed my broken heart, gave me a new start when I needed it, took me further than I would've ever gone on my own, helped me face and overcome things and people from my past, and has been faithful to help me grow in whatever season I was in. He continues to help me walk through new doors of opportunity. Now, He's helped me write my first book.

Here's the reality. If you want to be able to overcome things in your life, there's no way to do that fully and long-term without God. God sent His only Son Jesus to die for you. He not only died for your sins, but He overcame death and rose again on the third day. This is the key to how you can overcome. It's accepting what Jesus did on the Cross and inviting Him now to come and live in your heart. Who else has died for you? Who else never changes, loves you unconditionally, and will continue to? Who else is eternal and will never leave you?

If you've been led to believe lies about God, you're not alone in that, but it's time now to face the truth. God really is good. He really does love you. He really is the answer. People may have hurt you, but that wasn't from God. God is a safe place to put your trust and hope. If you feel a tugging on your heart now and have never accepted Jesus as your Savior and want to, please say a prayer to God now asking Him to come into your life and into your heart. Say whatever is on your heart. If you feel like you don't know what to say, pray the following: "Lord, I now know that You love me. I know that You sent Jesus to die for my sins. Forgive me for my sins and for rejecting You in the past. I choose today to turn away from my old ways. I invite You into my life and into my heart. I choose You on this day, Lord."

This is called salvation or getting saved. This truly is the best decision that you can make in your life. This is the key to having the ability to overcome anything. Salvation is the first tool. Once that's done, there are many other tools that a Christian can use. They're like weapons. There's a war going on in this world. It's a war of good versus evil, God versus Satan. Satan is loose, and there's much evil in the world. It's crucial to use spiritual tools, the weapons that are available to us from God, in order to have victory over evil and anything that may come against us.

Ephesians 6:10-18 (NKJV) discusses some of the tools listed here. Particularly, I want to mention verse 12. It says, "For we do not wrestle against flesh and blood, but against principalities, against powers, against the rulers of the darkness of this age, against spiritual hosts of wickedness in the heavenly places." We don't wrestle or fight against flesh and blood. In other words, our battle isn't against the humans that we see; it's against spiritual forces of darkness – Satan and his demons. We cannot use physical weapons against spiritual forces. We must use spiritual tools / weapons in order to be victorious.

Each of the spiritual tools or weapons that I'm going to share with you are ones that I've personally used. They helped me overcome whatever I was facing in that season of life. They work. I didn't make them up; they're in Scripture, and I've found each one to be powerful.

The words of a person's testimony are the second powerful tool. Testimony is simply telling others what God has done in your life. Think about someone who testifies in a court case. He or she is a witness to what has happened. That's what this book is all about: testimony. I'm sharing with you what has happened in order that you can also overcome by the same power that I have overcome. This is the power of Jesus Christ working in my life through His Holy Spirit that came to live inside of me at salvation.

I choose each day to live for God or for myself. The more I yield to God and His power in my life, the better my life gets.

Tools for Overcoming

Living for myself kept me miserable, making bad choices, and then reaping the consequences. Now, I have new life. These are the words of my testimony. What is your testimony? Do you have a testimony? When did you last share it? Not only will it be easier for you to overcome in your life as you speak and remind yourself of what God has done in your life, but it will also help others overcome whatever they may be facing.

Also, how often are you listening to other people's testimonies? Whether online or in person, hearing other people's testimonies will help inspire you, build your faith, and remind you that nothing is impossible for God.

The blood of Jesus is the third powerful weapon. How does one use it? For me, I love to take communion. Some call this "holy communion" or "The Lord's Supper." Shortly before Jesus went to the Cross, He had a special meal with His disciples. Often, people call this "The Last Supper." It was the last recorded meal that Jesus had before He went to the Cross. They had bread and wine. Jesus said that the bread represented His body, which would be broken for them. The wine represented His blood, which would be shed for them. He told them to do this act of eating the bread and drinking the wine often in remembrance of Him.

I've taken communion many places. I've taken it at home, at a restaurant, in an airport, and many other places. Basically, every day is a good day to do this. It honors Jesus when we remember what He did for us. There's also power in this for us when we do this.

I've used a variety of things. I try to use the purest items that are available. I've bought these items from a Christian bookstore or online. I've also bought no sugar added grape juice and unsalted crackers from the grocery store. I've also used bread served at a restaurant and whatever else was on hand. I had the privilege of having communion when I was in Israel in 2016 in the Garden of Gethsemane, where Jesus prayed before He was arrested and went to the Cross. That was a special moment.

The name of Jesus is one of my favorite spiritual weapons. This is the fourth tool. Usually, the first thing I say when I wake up and the last thing I say before I go to bed is simply "Jesus." There's no name greater than His. Forces of darkness hate this

I Found God Outside of Church

name. I don't need to say a long prayer; I simply acknowledge Who and what are most important by this simple act. Not only does it help me keep focused on what is most important, but it also causes forces of darkness (Satan and his demons) to flee.

The fifth tool is the Word of God. During the hardest time in my life, there were certain verses that gave me hope, new life, and strength to go on. When I couldn't sleep at night, I had a particular verse that I would meditate on. Isaiah 26:3 (NLT) says, "You will keep in perfect peace all who trust in you, all whose thoughts are fixed on you!" As I did what this verse says, I began to sleep much better. If you don't have a Bible, I encourage you to invest in one today. As long as you're not in a country where they're illegal, you can find one at most bookstores. If you have a smart phone, I would also download an application of the Bible. There are several good ones that are free, easy to use, and have many translations available. The words in the Bible aren't just words. They're full of wisdom and of answers to problems. They're also healing. The more you get in the Word of God, the stronger you will become.

The sixth tool is prayer. Prayer is simply talking to God. If you don't know what to say, that's ok. Start with that. "God, I really don't know what to say, but here's what I'm going through." Just be real with Him. He already knows everything, but He wants to hear from you. He cares and wants you to let Him into your situation. He wants to help you and provide for you. He wants to comfort you. He wants to guide you. Talk to Him regularly. Ask Him what His thoughts are about the situation. Then, pause to listen for Him. Treat it like a two-sided conversation. You might be surprised at how He speaks to you. I'll share more on this in the next chapter.

The seventh tool is going to church, Bible study, or a small Christian group. Going is part of growing. We're not meant to do this Christian journey alone. Having other people to relate to and connect with spiritually is important. Hearing good teaching and great testimonies will also give you strength to overcome.

The eighth tool is Christian music. It's important to listen to music that's full of hope, truth, and encouragement. Christian music can give you strength and help you focus on what's important. There's good and bad Christian music out there. Listen long enough to find some songs and artists that resonate with you. Look online or ask someone what local Christian radio stations are available in your area. Download a music application on your phone, and find a Christian station on it. Your day and your mood will be much more peaceful if you're filling your mind and heart with music about God, truth, overcoming, etc.

During my very dark season, there was one song that I used to listen to night after night when I had trouble sleeping: "In Christ Alone" sung by Keith and Kristyn Getty. This song reminded me where my strength comes from.

The ninth tool is daily devotionals. This is an expansion of the fifth tool – the Word of God. Devotionals are great because they help explain what a verse or passage is about. They help you apply what you're reading to your daily life. They take a segment of the Bible and break it down into a daily portion to focus on. I love devotionals. I've enjoyed using one in the morning and a different one in the evening. Ask a Christian friend that you relate to what he or she is using. Go to your local Christian bookstore and find one there. Pray before you go, and ask God to point you to the right one.

The tenth tool is thankfulness. It's really hard to have a bad day when you start the day thankful. "Enter his gates with thanksgiving and his courts with praise; give thanks to him and praise his name" (Psalm 100:4, NIV). One way to get in God's presence is thankfulness. I've found that I need to daily let God know what I'm thankful for. This sets a tone for the rest of my day. There are always things to be thankful for. I set a reminder in my phone for a certain time each morning to remind myself to stop what I'm doing and take a few minutes to let God know what I'm thankful for. This will guard you against self-pity, bad attitudes, jealousy, thinking the grass is greener elsewhere, etc.

Trust me that no matter how bad things might seem in your life, someone has it much worse than you. If you have easy access to unlimited, clean, drinking water, you're doing much better than most in the world. If you own more than one pair of shoes, you're also doing much better than most in the world. If you're able to see colors, have you ever thanked God that you're not color-blind? There are so many things to be thankful for.

The eleventh tool is speaking in tongues, which is a heavenly language. This coincides with prayer. The power of this tool cannot be underestimated. Paul, who wrote the majority of

I Found God Outside of Church

the books we read in the New Testament of the Bible, said he did this more than anyone else (1 Corinthians 14:18). I knew one pastor who counseled people. He advised anyone struggling with depression to speak in tongues for a half hour or more each day. The more they spoke in tongues, the more they came out of depression. When we speak in a heavenly language, we're speaking over ourselves and our lives God's thoughts. What could be more powerful?

Maybe you're saying that you don't have this gift. Pray and ask God for it. Pray without ceasing. Pray and seek it until you get it. If you're not in a church that exercises this gift or understands it, seek God and see if it's time to go to a church where they've dug deeper into the things of God. This tool will change your life. When we use this, we're pushing the powers of darkness back and walking in victory in our lives at a greater level. I'll discuss my testimony regarding this gift in chapter 17.

This list isn't comprehensive, but it's meant to help you go further in your spiritual journey. The more you seek God, the more you will find Him. The more time you spend with Him, the more He will transform you.

Which of these tools will you begin to use today? What tool not listed here is God calling you to use? Is there something that you were doing that you set aside that God wants you to begin again? What do you need to give up in order to have time for your relationship with God?

Next, I'll share one of the things that has transformed my life more than anything else: how I learned to hear from the Creator of the universe and how you can too!

14
Knowing the Voice of God

What do people mean when they say they heard from God, or God led them to do something? Have you ever heard from God? Does He speak in an audible voice?

I went with a friend to hear a Christian speaker in 2012. The speaker shared that she had gone to a women's conference, where each of them had gotten in a corner and spent 20 minutes being still and quiet while they focused on Jesus being there with them. The speaker thought this would be impossible. She didn't think she could sit still and focus for that long. Each person was given a focus word that would help her focus on Jesus. Although she was skeptical at first, the speaker said that she really felt the presence of God during that time and didn't want that time to end. She began to spend time each day being quiet before God, and she said that it changed her life.

Not too long after I heard this testimony, I went to another Christian gathering in someone's home. We were given a sheet of paper with instructions when we arrived. Basically, the time was meant to be with God. We were all to remain quiet, unless we felt led to play an instrument in worship.

This was the second time I heard about being quiet and spending time with God. I felt led to go over to the dining room table. Once I sat down in one of the chairs, the thought came to me to kneel on the floor, so I did. God really showed up in such a special way. I could sense His presence with me. It was wonderful and also emotional. I believe He was healing me from some emotional baggage.

I knew that I needed to start taking 20 minutes each day to spend with God while simply being quiet. I began by turning off all distractions – television, phone, etc. I would put my phone on silent, yet I would set my alarm for 20 minutes later. Even time can try to be a distraction when you sit still. How long has it been? When can I go do this? What if I'm late for that? I set my alarm so that not even time was an issue.

Because the mind can try to wander, I also used a focus word. Peace was usually my focus word. God gives that peace that surpasses all understanding. He is peace. He's also love, so sometimes, I would use love as my focus word.

It's normal for the mind to start wandering to what needs to be done for the day, what's for lunch, what bill needs to be paid, etc. I've found that it's ok for all of that stuff to come up during that time with God. It's like a transference. I'm transferring all the cares of the day over to God and receiving His peace instead. We're supposed to cast our cares on God, but how often do we actually do this (I Peter 5:7)? I'm always so much lighter after I spend this time with God.

I continued to spend this time with God each day, and He began to speak to me. A thought would come – sometimes about myself, sometimes about another person. It was gentle yet powerful. He would speak to me right in the area that I needed. One time, He told me that I needed to forgive someone. Another time, He kept bringing a former coworker to mind. I reached out to her, and she was really having a hard time. I told her that God had put her on my heart; she said that she was glad that God was thinking of her.

When a person invites Jesus Christ into his or her life, the Holy Spirit of Jesus Christ then comes and lives inside that person. So, when God speaks, it's actually often coming from inside that person – where the Holy Spirit is. For me, it's a matter of getting my own thoughts quiet, so that I can hear from Him, who lives inside of me. It's like I'm tuning in to Him.

Thoughts can come from ourselves, Satan, or God. I usually ask God to quiet my thoughts and any thoughts that Satan would want to speak, so that I can clearly hear from God.

I've found that it's important to "test the spirit" that speaks to me. Basically, when a thought comes to you, test to see where it's from. Is it coming from the Holy Spirit or a demonic spirit? Scripture gives us a way to know for sure whether or not the spirit that is speaking to you / dropping a thought to you is from God (Holy Spirit) or not. After a thought or voice speaks to you, ask that thought or voice, "Did Jesus Christ come in the flesh?" This test is found in I John 4:2. If the answer is yes, then you know it's from the Lord. If the answer is no, then you know that it's a demonic spirit.

Many times, people feel guilty for having a wrong thought. I don't think that you should have guilt for a bad thought coming to you. There are times when Satan can drop bad thoughts into your mind. It's what you do with the thought when it comes that matters the most. Do you shut down the thought and resist it if it's bad, or do you entertain the thought and go further with it in your mind? Satan is hoping that it will sound good to you and that you will take his bait and continue with the thought. He then hopes that these thoughts will take root, grow, and eventually, turn into words and actions.

The biggest key to learning the voice of God is simply listening. It's hard to hear someone when you're talking. Prayer is good, important, and has its place, but listening and being quiet are keys to getting to know God's voice.

If you never listen to a person, how could you ever recognize their voice? It's no different with God. Setting aside time is really all you have to do. He will show up and do the rest.

You may have powerful moments when God speaks to you over the sound of everything else. He may speak to you in a church service or through a Christian speaker on the radio or some other avenue, but you don't have to wait for those moments. You can hear from Him directly every day. That's right; the Creator of the universe wants to spend time with you, yes you, every single day.

It can be uncomfortable to do something new and may take some time to incorporate this into your daily routine. It will be more than worth any time spent and will change your life for the better. This is one of the things that has grown me the most spiritually. Spending this time daily is what helped me get comfortable with knowing the voice of God.

Another thing that helped me as I spent this time with God was to close my eyes and picture Jesus in front of me wanting to talk to me and spend time with me. Picturing Him helps me get focused on Him. There's no right or wrong answer as to what He looks like. It's not like we have a photograph to go by. Let God give you an image as you picture Him.

When I first started spending this time being quiet, I would get comfortable on the floor and sit Indian style. I did that for a while. Eventually, I started laying down on the floor when I would spend this time with God. Do whatever you are led to do. God works with each of us individually.

It's ok if you occasionally fall asleep during this time. I've had people tell me that they feel guilty for falling asleep reading

I Found God Outside of Church

the Bible. God gives a peace unlike any other. If you occasionally fall asleep, there's nothing to feel guilty about.

I used to have it perfectly quiet during this time. Eventually, I started having some worship music playing in the background. Currently, I'm not playing music during that time. Do what you feel led to do.

Once, I was in a small group, and we took some time to focus on Jesus and listen for Him. I told the group to with their eyes closed picture Jesus in front of them, wanting to spend time with them. One guy later said that he couldn't seem to sense Jesus in front of him. He said that he tilted his head back, and then, he could sense Jesus. That's great! Do whatever God leads you to do. One girl that was there said that she could sense and hear angels singing in the room with us. Enjoy God's presence. He loves spending time with us.

During this time, I've had many different experiences. When you think of your time spent with a person, each time is different. It's no different with Jesus. Sometimes, it seems like I'm mostly unloading all of the stuff that has tried to stick to me from the world. Other times, it seems I'm being healed internally. I've been led to reach out and touch Jesus by faith. The Word of God says that by His wounds or by His stripes, we are healed (Isaiah 53:5). Many times, I reach out to touch by faith the wounds that Jesus experienced in His hands, feet, or side. I want to receive all that is available to me. Often times, there are things inside of us that need healing that we aren't even aware of. God wants to go into those places, heal us, restore us, and make us new.

He is trustworthy. Let Him into those deeper places. Sometimes, it's emotional to allow someone into that pain, but the healing makes it worth it.

Sometimes, I spend that time resting in His presence. I never know what the time will be like; I just know that I always come out better. The longer I continued to spend this time with God, the more comfortable I got with knowing His voice. Now, I'm comfortable hearing from Him and knowing that it's Him wherever I am.

One time, God told me to minister to this man in our Sunday school class and tell him to get rid of the anger in his life. I hesitated to say this to him, but God kept saying the same thing to me, so I finally gave in and told him what God had said. After telling the man that God loves him but wants him to get rid of the anger, the man was eager to tell me that he had been very angry lately. He seemed glad that God knew what he was struggling with.

Another time, I was in a church, and we were praying for a man. With my eyes closed, I kept seeing an image of a cross on the man's chest. I told him what I saw, and he told me that that was truly from God. He said that he has a cross necklace that he almost wore that night.

God has also trusted me with a prophetic word for one of His people regarding something yet to happen. I've had a couple people confirm to me later that what I spoke to them did come about. That was all from hearing and knowing the voice of God. I don't know these things on my own.

I personally have never heard God in an audible voice. I've only met a couple of people who have heard Him audibly.

In the beginning, a lot of healing was taking place for me. I treasure the times of reaching out and touching Jesus. The power I felt when I did so and the peace that washed over me are indescribable. Basically, I was getting out of the natural and tuning in to the supernatural, the unseen realm.

I think of it as tuning in to a radio station with an old radio that has a knob that you turn. You're trying to get to where there are no muffled noises. All you want to hear is that station. In this case, all you want to hear is God. This isn't a difficult thing to do. The hardest part is simply setting the time aside. God will do the rest.

God isn't forceful, but He is powerful. When He speaks, He gives clarity. He gives peace. He gives direction. He comforts. He encourages. He sets us free. He heals. He inspires. He strengthens. He guides and does so many other amazing things.

Sometimes, we get to a place where we have no one and nothing else to distract us away from God. That was the case for me when I moved to Savannah in 2011. I was hungry for more of God, particularly in that season of my life.

I once was told by a prison chaplain that the first thing that most inmates in the U.S. ask for after they're incarcerated is a Bible. I find that very interesting. Is it because they know in the depths of their being that God is the answer? Is it because they

I Found God Outside of Church

need hope, and they internally know where to go?

When I began to listen for God, I was in a lot of pain, and I didn't have anyone else to go to with that pain. God is always available to us. He wants us to come to a place where we get to know Him for ourselves. He doesn't want us to just know what others have said about Him. Frankly, a lot of that might be wrong. Church experiences definitely don't reflect all of who He is. In fact, one time, God said something to me that I will never forget. He said, "There's very little of me in today's churches."

I encourage you to get to know God and hear His voice for yourself. There's nothing bad about Him. He's so loving and kind. He's patient. He works with you right where you are with no judgement. He will be the best friend you've ever had. He knows all of the wrong I've done, yet He chooses to spend time with me. And He enjoys spending that time with me. He's so good. He'll never get tired of you. He always wants to hear from you. He delights in spending time with you. There's always enough of Him for you. Nothing you bring to Him will shock Him. Nothing is too big or too hard for Him.

God wants to do something mighty on the inside of you. Let Him. It will bring the relief that you've longed for. And it may just begin with you stopping everything else and listening for His voice.

There was one time that I heard the voice of God when I wasn't sure that I wanted to hear what He had to say. This would be a greater test of faith than I had ever experienced.

15
Test of Faith

In early 2015, my faith was tested. That night at church, we prayed for a man that had been struggling financially and had accepted a job out of state. They took up an offering for him and prayed for him, as he was about to head out of town that very night.

I was on the way home from this service when I heard, "Give him your car." I thought to myself, "Umm, I don't think I heard that right." I heard again, "Give him your car." I said, "Lord, if that's You, I need You to make this clear to me."

I knew what God was telling me to do, but this involved a level of faith that I definitely had never exercised before. I lived alone and only had the one vehicle. This was my way to work, church, etc. I didn't see how I had any other means of transportation.

The vehicle I owned had given me some problems in the last couple of years. I had had the transmission rebuilt and had a few other things done. It was a 2001 Chevrolet Camaro that was 14 years old and had about 150,000 miles on it. It was the only new car I had ever purchased. I had bought it from the dealership and had taken care of it.

The body of the car was in great condition. I had had a few people ask me in the last few years if I was willing to sell it. Although it was older, it looked pretty good for its age. The exterior was a light pewter, metallic color. The windows were tinted, and it also had removable T-tops.

So, I'm on the way home, and I know what God is telling me, but it's way out of my comfort zone. God has a way though of preparing us for the things He will ask us to do. Like I said, my car had been having some problems in the past year. I had had it worked on for several days more than once. There was a sweet, young couple from my church that had loaned me one of their vehicles when my car was being worked on. They were happy to help. The husband said that someone had loaned him a vehicle when he needed one when he was in college. Another time, when my car was being worked on, the guy that I was dating had given me rides each day to and from work. God

I Found God Outside of Church

brought to mind these people who had helped me.

The man who was headed out of state had an older truck that seemed to break down regularly. I knew what God was asking of me, but I began to question how this would work for me. "What will I do without a car? How will I get to work?" I started jumping ahead in my mind, but God wanted me to just take things one step and one day at a time.

First, was I going to obey and yield to what God was asking of me? With great discomfort, I chose to say yes to God and to trust Him to take care of me. I can't really explain how I was able to do this, except that God gave me the strength to. God told me to call the man and tell him that I had something I wanted to give him before he left town. God didn't want me to tell him what it was though. He said to have the man come to me to receive the gift.

Church had run late, and I lived about 45 minutes from the church. It was already late in the evening. I called the man, and I could tell that he was busily trying to get out of town and still needed to see his family. I told him what God told me to say and nothing more. I sensed that he had a lot of things pulling at him, and I wasn't sure that he would even come get the car.

I could tell that his family was also pulling him in different directions. I told him the area that I lived in, and he said that he would call me when he was on the way. Some time passed, and I didn't think that he was going to come. Not only was God requiring action from me, but He was also requiring action from this man. God had a gift waiting for him, but would he bother to come when he was so busy and trying to get out of town?

While I waited, I began to think of a few things that I could put in the car for him. It was winter time, and I didn't know if he even had anywhere to stay once he got out of town. I put a pillow and blanket in the car for him, just in case.

He eventually called me for detailed directions. He lived about an hour away and didn't have any kind of GPS. As he got closer, I was trying to explain how to find my apartment complex. He was lost and had made a wrong turn. It was hard to figure out where he was.

Eventually, he made it! I was standing outside waiting for him. When he pulled into the parking lot, his truck had smoke billowing out from underneath the hood. His truck had barely made it to my apartment.

I then explained what God had told me to do. We talked for a bit, and then, I gave him the keys and told him that the car was now his. He was thankful. I prayed for him, and then he left in what used to be my car.

By this time, it was after midnight, and I didn't know how I would get to church in the morning. I knew that his truck had run its course and that I wasn't to use it. I was trying not to freak out. God told me to just take things one day at a time. He said that all I needed to think about for now was a way to get to church in the morning. This all happened on a Saturday night. God said that I should set my alarm and text my friend in the morning to see if she could pick me up for church.

So, when I went to bed that night, I no longer owned a vehicle. It was a very strange feeling. I was way out of my elements.

I texted my friend the next morning and said that I had no way to church. I didn't go into any details. She said that I could use one of their vehicles that day. She picked me up that morning and took me to get the vehicle.

I explained to her what had happened. She was very interested in what I had to say and said that she would talk to her husband about me using one of their vehicles in the meantime.

I was eager to start looking for a car that very day, but God told me to wait. He said to wait 7 days before I did anything.

Waiting can be very hard. I was eager to get this "problem" solved. I didn't like not knowing what I would be driving or when I would be getting a vehicle.

Waiting isn't always fun, but it serves a purpose. "But those who wait on the Lord shall renew their strength; They shall mount up with wings like eagles, They shall run and not be weary, They shall walk and not faint" (Isaiah 40:31, NKJV). Waiting makes us stronger. God wants us stronger. He also wants to show us who He is. A lot of times, we put needless pressure or worry on ourselves when He's got us. He's never failed us and never will. Do we think that He might fail us now? Do we think that it's all up to us? Do we forget that He's with us and for us? There's nothing that He wouldn't do for us. He did give us Jesus after all.

I Found God Outside of Church

I explained to my friend that had loaned me the vehicle that God wanted me to wait a week before I did anything. She and her husband seemed ok with it.

It was hard not to get online that week to look at vehicles. I didn't know if I would buy new or used. Would it be a car or an SUV? Would I buy from an individual or a dealer? Waiting wasn't easy, but I did refrain from looking for those 7 days.

Finally, the week passed, and I prayed and asked God for direction. He then told me that it was time to start looking for a new vehicle.

Although getting a new vehicle sounds great, I didn't think that I was financially ready for a car note. If I passed a test on my job for a certification and did a few other things, I would be eligible for a raise in the next few months. I wanted to possibly get a new vehicle after the pay raise.

But that was my thinking; that wasn't God's thinking. He wanted me to live as though I already had the raise. That's what faith looks like. It's not just believing; it's believing to the point of taking action. It's taking action before the thing has come to pass. I wasn't used to that.

I began to see how little faith I'd had and used throughout my life. I was always trying to wait until everything made sense. But there's no faith in that. "And without faith it is impossible to please God" (Hebrews 11:6, NIV).

As I began to look for a vehicle, I knew that I didn't want a two-door car anymore. I also wanted a car that was a little better on gas mileage. I didn't need anything too large. I just wanted a small to medium-sized, 4-door sedan. I ruled out the Toyota Corolla. That was what I was currently driving that belonged to my friend. I didn't like the way that it sat. A process of elimination began. I thought that maybe I would get a Hyundai.

For some reason, I couldn't seem to stop looking at Nissans. I seemed stuck on the Nissan Sentra. I started asking God to show me what car He wanted me to get. I asked him for a sign. Not too long after that, I was headed through a large store parking lot. As I drove up the aisle, there were not 1, not 2, but 3 Nissan Sentras right there together in that aisle!

If you want a sign, ask God for one. Sometimes, we're more in tune with God than we realize. He was leading me through the process even though I wasn't talking to Him every second of that process.

It was two weeks before I purchased a new car – a Nissan Sentra. It was fully loaded with all options: leather, heated seats; sunroof; the nicer sound system; et cetera. It was a huge upgrade from my 14-year-old car. Just think, I could've easily ignored what God wanted me to do that night when He told me to give my car away. I guess I could've kept driving around a 14-year-old vehicle.

I never went a day without a good vehicle to drive in those two weeks before I bought the new car. God also enabled me to bless someone else in this process. My old car was an upgrade for that man, and it took him further than his truck would have. He later told me that he did end up pulling over to sleep in the car that night that he left town. The heat in his old truck didn't work, but the car's heat was working. He also said that he used the pillow and the blanket that night.

Acting in faith and obedience brought my upgrade. I wonder how many upgrades we've missed out on because we didn't trust God enough to let go of what we had. I think that many times, we're waiting until we can see that the upgrade is on the way before we let go of what we have. That's not God's thinking though. He's waiting for us to let go of what we have (faith in action), and then, He gives us the upgrade.

This is definitely an area that I'm still growing in. It wasn't easy to give my car away, but I thank God that He helped me to be obedient.

By the way, I got the raise on my job at the earliest date that I was eligible for it. My first car note on my interest-free loan wasn't due for approximately six weeks, and I received the raise right around the time that my first car note was due.

When did you last exercise faith? What is God asking you to let go of today? What upgrade awaits you?

Growing in faith was great; next, God wanted to teach me about the power of words.

16
The Power of Words

"Sticks and stones may break my bones, but words will never hurt me." I heard this saying when I was a child; I probably even said it. That phrase is a lie straight from the pit of hell.

Words have power. I'm still learning just how much power they have. When my mom criticized me when I was growing up, it hurt. When kids at school teased me or played a joke on me, it hurt. And I'm sure that my words have also hurt others.

God has been teaching me that what we say is important. Adam, the first man, got to name the animals. We're still calling them the same names that Adam gave those first animals.

When God spoke at creation, things happened. Why would we think that it would be any different when we, who have Him inside of us, speak?

If you wanted to remember things that people have said over the years that have hurt you, I'm sure it wouldn't be difficult to do. Hopefully, you've forgiven them and don't dwell on those words.

When I was in Brazil, one of our team members was commanding the clouds to move so that we could see a famous statue in the distance. Jesus said that we can command a mountain to move, and as long as we have a tiny amount of faith, the mountain will move.

Our words have the power to move mountains! At some point, I decided to start trying this with weather. I decided that I didn't have anything to lose. One day when it was raining, I didn't want to get soaked going to my car, so I commanded the rain to stop. Within one second, it hadn't stopped, so I figured that nothing was going to happen. I gave up easily.

Later, God said to me, "You didn't wait for it to stop." So, I did the same thing again another day. This time, I waited. The rain began to die down.

Since that day, I've commanded the rain to divert away from where I was traveling several times. It's been amazing to see the results. I've seen the rain stop many times after I've told it to. Our words have power, and we have more authority than we've known.

I Found God Outside of Church

I declared before I went to Alaska in 2017 that the weather was going to be sunny and warm. One Alaskan city that I visited gets approximately 141 inches of rain per year. The day I was there, it was sunny and warm. The tour guide said that they only get days like that maybe 5% of the time. I just smiled because I knew why the weather was nice that day.

I went on three different flight tours while I was in Alaska. One was in a helicopter in one city; another was in a float plane in another city; and the third was in a ski plane in a third city. I was told in advance that all of the flights and tours were contingent upon the weather. The weather in most of the cities that I visited can change drastically from one hour to the next. Not a single tour or flight was cancelled. I had clear, sunny weather for every flight.

One tour was in a ski plane over Mt. Denali. The pilot said that it was one of the clearest days he's ever seen around the mountain. Often, the clouds have prevented a good view of the peaks. We got to land on a glacier and get out and walk around. It was 60 degrees. I didn't even need a coat. One girl up there was wearing shorts! Our words have power.

I've gotten more and more comfortable with declaring things and expecting things to happen accordingly. When hurricane Irma was expected to come to my area in 2017, they issued a mandatory evacuation at one point for much of the area near where I lived. I was on the outskirts of that evacuation zone. Many people were glued to the television trying to figure out what the storm was doing. Many were also talking about evacuating on social media. I simply heard God say, "Stay." So, I made no evacuation plans.

I knew that if God told me to stay, He knew what He was talking about. Many people were getting pulled in many different directions because they kept watching the news and relying on the meteorologists to tell them what was happening. The storm changed direction many times.

I had total peace about staying home that weekend. In fact, my work shut down due to the evacuation, and I got some paid time off work, which was a blessing.

I declared out loud that I would not lose electrical power and that I would experience no flooding where I lived. Guess what? My electricity never went out, and it didn't flood at all

The Power of Words

where I lived. In fact, around the time that they were saying that the storm was at its peak, I went outside on my patio. The sun began to shine through the clouds at me right where I was standing. I just smiled. It seemed like God was smiling down on me in that moment.

Some people evacuated and enjoyed seeing family or friends. Others tried to avoid the storm by evacuating, but the storm followed them and hit the area where they evacuated to.

We have access to the Creator of the universe Who knows all. I recommend going to Him for direction instead of the television or social media. There's no need to panic when the rest of the world does. God said to stay, so I did, and all was well. If He had told me to leave, then I would've done that.

I then exercised the authority that I have inside of me over the weather and "Irma" because of my relationship with Jesus Christ and what He did on the Cross. He defeated death and hell and rose again from the dead. The same power that rose Him from the dead now lives inside of me. I have power and authority. You have that same power if you're a Christian. Jesus was able to stop the wind and the waves; so can we.

"Death and life are in the power of the tongue, and those who love it will eat its fruit" (Proverbs 18:21, NKJV). Be careful what you say. If you say that it's going to be a long day, guess what you will get? A long day is what you'll have. If you say that you have a chronic disease, guess what you will continue to have? A chronic disease.

One day, as I was on the way to work, I said out loud in my car, "This is going to be one of the best days I've had in a long time." Guess what happened? I got a cash award that day on my job, and it was one of the best days I had had in a long time. Our words have power.

Several years ago, one of my family members was a senior in high school. His math teacher told him that he was two points short of passing and that there was no way he could graduate. He texted me and told me what the teacher had said. Something rose up inside of me on a Sunday night, and I began to say out loud, "He will graduate. He will walk across that stage with the rest of his class."

Jesus said that He is the way, the truth, and the life. He is the way. There is always a way. I refused to accept that this

I Found God Outside of Church

family member had come this far and was so close to the finish line, and now, this teacher is telling him that there's no way? Maybe she doesn't know the God that I know. There is always a way!

I know for a fact that my words have power, and the words that I spoke in faith shifted something spiritually. The next day, I got a text saying that the very teacher who had said that there was no way he could graduate has now decided to give him the two points and is now passing him through that class. He would now be graduating! This was less than 24 hours after I declared that he would in fact graduate.

God can even change the heart of an unbeliever. I don't know if this person knew God or not. But what I do know is that our words have power. Don't take no for an answer if you know that you shouldn't. Sometimes, we're getting whatever Satan wants to send to us because we don't stand up to him or speak up. Satan is always trying to steal. He wanted to steal this graduation, but I refused to be silent or to back down with my words. I praise God for the victory that we have because of what His Son Jesus did for us.

Another time, I was at home getting ready for work. Suddenly, I felt a tormenting pain in my stomach area. I felt nauseous. To me, that's one of the worst ways to be sick. I had things to do that day and didn't want to miss work or miss the things that I needed to do after work. I chose to not accept the symptoms of what I was feeling. I began to speak the opposite of what I felt. I said, "I will not get sick at my stomach. I am healthy. I will not miss work today. I refuse sickness."

I also prayed to God and examined myself before Him. I heard Him say that I needed to forgive someone that had recently hurt me. God told me that I should text that person and tell him that I forgive him, so I did. I received a reply asking what I was forgiving him for. I simply said that it was for anything he had said or done that had hurt me.

Then, I felt like God wanted me to worship Him. I put some worship music on, and within 30 minutes of the symptoms having come, they disappeared. I literally started jumping up and down in my living room 30 minutes after I had felt like I was about to vomit.

Just because pain or symptoms come to you, that doesn't

mean that you have to accept them. In this instance, there was also a person that I needed to forgive. This tells me that this is how Satan had access to inflict me with something. Anytime there's an area in our lives that's not in accordance with God's Word, this gives Satan an open door to us. "Be alert and of sober mind. Your enemy the devil prowls around like a roaring lion looking for someone to devour. Resist him, standing firm in the faith" (1 Peter 5:8-9, NIV). We're to resist Satan when he comes. How do you know it's him? If it involves stealing anything from you, then it's him. If the situation is trying to steal your health, your joy, your finances, your family, or anything else good, then it's more than likely from Satan. If it involves killing, destroying, lying, or deception, then it's also probably Satan.

We can't live any way that we want though and think that there will be no consequences. If you spend your money on unnecessary things and then don't have enough money to pay your bills, that's not Satan, that's you. Satan may be influencing your thinking and decisions, but ultimately, you are choosing how to spend your money.

Also, if you're out of God's will in any area of your life, Satan has a legal right to you because of that sin or disobedience. It's always wise to examine yourself before the Lord and ask Him to show you anything that you may need to change. David, one of the famous kings of Israel who defeated the giant Goliath, said in Psalms 139:23-24, NKJV: "Search me, O God, and know my heart; Try me, and know my anxieties; And see if there is any wicked way in me, And lead me in the way everlasting."

"My dear brothers and sisters, take note of this: Everyone should be quick to listen, slow to speak and slow to become angry" (James 1:19, NIV). The reason why we should be slow to speak is that we need to think about what we say before we release those words. God wants us to understand the weight of our words.

If you say or believe words such as, "I'm a failure," guess what you will probably be? No matter how you feel, choose to speak words of life over yourself and others. Words have power; choose them carefully.

If a person says, "I'm disabled," guess what he or she will be? No matter what is going on physically, always choose to

I Found God Outside of Church

speak perfect health over yourself. Don't give Satan any access to you by coming into agreement with symptoms, feelings, or even a diagnosis by a doctor. Symptoms and feelings can be fickle and temporary. Diagnoses can also be wrong. Satan may be giving you some temporary symptoms in the hope that you'll accept a diagnosis that you have something wrong. Once you declare that you have it, you really will have it.

Now, I want you to think about a time that someone said something to you that positively changed your life. Several years ago, I was in a church service. A woman got up and started singing a song. Then, she paused, looked directly at me, and told me that I needed to be writing and that people needed to know what I've been through. This woman didn't know me, but the God inside of her did. She confirmed a calling on my life, and it was powerful when she spoke those words. Her words helped move me closer to action.

What have you been saying lately? What things do you need to stop saying? What should you start saying instead?

Teaching me the power of words was great, but God still wanted to take me deeper.

17

Digging Deeper

Whatever you've learned up to this point about God and spiritual things, I guarantee you that there's more. I want to share in further detail about one of the tools for overcoming that I mentioned in chapter 13.

I grew up in a church where the people there definitely did not speak in tongues. Speaking in tongues is one of many gifts that God gives believers (I Corinthians 12:4-11). It's a heavenly language that can sound very unusual. I never heard it talked about from a pastor or teacher in all of my years growing up in church or being in a "Christian" school. I do remember at an early age hearing two negative things about speaking in tongues. I once heard something like, "The crazy Pentecostals do that." I also heard, "They just jump up and do that without any interpretation." I didn't really know what either of those things meant. All I knew was that all I had heard about this topic was negative.

I never thought much about this subject for over twenty years in church. In my adult years, as I grew as a Christian and got used to hearing from God for myself, I became aware that there were a lot of things that I hadn't had any exposure to for over two decades in church. For instance, God is a God of miracles. He still does miracles today – whether that be physical healing, financial provision, or any number of other things. I didn't hear much about this aspect of God for many years. I also didn't learn in church how to listen for God's voice and how to hear from Him directly for myself. The Word says that God's sheep know His voice (John 10:27). I also didn't hear anything about prophecy (I Corinthians 14:1). Yet, as I grew in my relationship with God, I learned that there was a whole bunch that I hadn't been exposed to in church.

First, I had to be freed from some thinking and mindsets that were wrong and were very closed-minded. Bit by bit, God opened me up to be able to receive more truth about Himself and about gifts that are available to Christians.

God doesn't give bad gifts, period. There's no such thing as God giving a bad gift. So even though the Bible says that

I Found God Outside of Church

speaking in tongues is a gift from God, I was told things that made me think negatively about this topic. How can this be? I now question how someone who doesn't even have the gift of speaking in tongues can talk positively or negatively about it. How do they know if it's good or bad when they don't have it for themselves?

I've learned that I was deceived about many things in church and also simply not exposed to many things, although I was in a supposedly "Christian" environment all my life, or so I thought I was.

God works in so many mysterious ways. He once appeared to Moses in a burning bush (Exodus 3). Just because I haven't had God appear to me that way, that doesn't mean that God doesn't do things like that or that it would be bad if He did. Yet, I've been in many Christian circles and churches that dismiss without question this topic of speaking in tongues.

I don't consider myself an expert on this subject, but I can tell you what I know and what I've experienced for myself.

At some point, God led me to a couple of different churches where I would hear people speaking in an unknown language during prayer or worship. It was strange to me. I had never been around this before and didn't really know what to think. It didn't seem to affect me much one way or the other.

As time went on, I seemed to be around it more and more. I got more comfortable with it the more I was exposed to it and the more I was growing in my relationship with God. However, I had no desire for it for myself. I regularly listened for God and heard from Him. I had grown a lot in my relationship with God and didn't feel like I was lacking anything in my walk with God.

But then, one day, God spoke to me and told me to have them lay hands on me at church and pray for me to receive the gift of speaking in tongues. I didn't feel like I needed it. I have the Holy Spirit. I hear from Him regularly. Why do I need this? But, I know that God only wants good for me. I trust Him, and as long as it's Him that's wanting something or directing something in my life, then I'm usually ok with it. In fact, I know that I must be obedient; otherwise, I won't have peace.

I went forward in the small church I was attending and went to the man that God directed me to go to. The man said that he couldn't give me the gift and that the gift is from God. He also said that he would be happy to pray for me to receive the gift. The church leadership and a few others that have the gift came forward, laid hands on me, and began praying for me in English and also in the heavenly language of tongues.

Some told me that when they got the gift, they heard the words in their head first. Others said that they saw the words. Others said that thoughts of words just came to them. Others said that it just started flowing out of them almost uncontrollably. They said that if anything came to me to just start moving my lips and to let it out.

It took some time and was uncomfortable, but eventually, one syllable came. And then, another syllable came. One woman was very encouraging. She would say, "You're doing it!" It helped to have them talk me through it and encourage me. God knows just what we need.

I started to feel the presence of God and began to cry good tears. I didn't understand fully what had happened or why, but I acted in obedience. I can't say that I started using this gift right away or that I even knew what to do with it. Some time passed before I really began to exercise the gift. A couple of people told me that the more I used it, the more it would grow.

One day as I was driving to work, God told me to speak in tongues the rest of the drive, so I did. All I know is that I felt lighter as I did. I arrived to work in the best mood ever. It seemed like the cares of the world had lifted from me, and joy came in their place. It was great. I could feel a big difference after those 15-20 minutes.

Another time, I was at home, and my washing machine was stuck on a particular cycle. It was one of those touch screen kinds. It had said for probably 15 minutes that there were only 8 minutes left. But the time on it wouldn't change, and it kept spinning and spinning. I tried turning the machine off and back on, unplugging it, etc. Nothing changed. I went over there and spoke the name of Jesus out loud. I know that there's power in that name. Yet, the remaining time on the machine still wouldn't change. Then, God told me to place my hand on the machine and to start speaking in tongues. I was frustrated at this point and willing to try anything. So, I did what He said, and immediately, the time changed on the machine, and it started working again!

I Found God Outside of Church

I now know that speaking in tongues is powerful. It's no wonder why Satan didn't want me to know about this or to think that it was good. I feel like I was robbed for many years by not knowing about this and other gifts that are available.

I want you to know that wherever you are spiritually, there's still so much more! Never be satisfied with what you have; there are always more truths, more revelations, and deeper things in the spiritual realm. The deeper I've gone into spiritual things, the better things have gotten.

I've heard several people talk about how they got the gift of speaking in tongues, and each story is unique and different – kind of like each person's story of how they came to know God and got saved. No two stories are alike. Some have said that the heavenly language flowed continually out of them for a long period of time, and it seemed they couldn't stop. Others have said that they got one or two syllables to start. Some received the gift at home; others received it at church.

For each person that reads this chapter, is a Christian, and desires this gift, the Holy Spirit is already inside of you. Ask God for this gift, open your mouth, and let Him speak through you. Try not to think; just yield to Him. Allow your world to be changed for the better. Your time is now!

18
What Are You Waiting For?

Are you living your life fully? Jesus said that was why He came. "I have come that they may have life, and have it to the full" (John 10:10, NIV). Before I surrendered every part of my heart to God, I wasn't really living. I wasn't enjoying life. I didn't know my purpose. Now, I continue to step out into the unknown. I go from adventure to adventure, from glory to glory.

What is it that you've been wanting to do for a long time? For years, I had wanted to go on an Alaskan cruise. I let money, not having the right person to go with me, and other factors stop me. But now, I finally did it, and it was one of the most memorable times of my life.

God definitely kept His word when He told me to imagine what else I would see if I continued to follow Him. I couldn't have come up with the things He's allowed me to see and do since then. I've been to Brazil, Israel, Alaska, Iceland, India, Uganda, South Africa, Canada, Mexico, and other places. I'll share some of what I wrote while on the Alaskan trip in 2017.

"I'm currently out on the open seas somewhere between Vancouver, Canada, and Ketchikan, Alaska, as I write this. This is my first full day on a 7-day, Alaskan cruise. I've been looking forward to this trip for quite some time. I've been wanting to go on an Alaskan cruise for several years. I'm blessed and thankful to be on this incredible journey.

This morning, I was seated with 4 strangers in the dining room for breakfast. Two were a middle-aged couple from Florida, and the other two were widowed women from Wisconsin. I was by far the youngest at the table by probably twenty to thirty years.

We began discussing various cruise lines and cruise experiences, as well as what shore excursions we've booked for this trip. The couple had not yet booked any excursions. I was asked what excursions I had booked, and I was eager to tell them that I'm going dog sledding on this trip. They were eager to know how much it costs. The two women said that they hadn't even seen that excursion as an option. One of the women sounded very interested in signing up for this. She asked what

I Found God Outside of Church

special clothing was needed. I said that you only need to dress warmly. The company recommended a hat and gloves, and they provide special boots that go over your regular shoes.

We had a great time while we shared various cruise experiences. I encouraged the woman to go for it, to book the dog sledding. I asked, "When will you ever be back in Alaska and have this opportunity again?" She was insistent that she hadn't brought the right clothes.

I explained that I've had coworkers that have vacation time available for use. One told me that she is waiting until she retires before she starts traveling places that she wants to see. She basically has the resources and time available to take off work, yet, she chooses not to do the things that she really desires to do.

It's time to live your life now. Tomorrow is not guaranteed on this earth. If you desire to do something, work towards it, and make it happen.

It's time to say no to fear and excuses. The one man at our table explained that older people always talk about the things that they didn't do, not the things that they did do. I explained that I've met people who have thought that they would start doing fun things and traveling after they retired. When they retired, their health declined, and it was then more difficult and less enjoyable to travel."

Here's some of what I wrote on my third day in Alaska in a place called Icy Strait Point:

"What an incredible day! At breakfast, before I even got off the ship, there was a whale right next to the ship. Then, as soon as we disembarked, we saw a beautiful bald eagle in a very tall tree near the ship. Next, we saw another whale before we were even off the dock! This place is so peaceful. It's definitely not commercialized like Ketchikan. I thoroughly enjoyed Ketchikan and the shopping there, but the sereneness of this place is amazing. I've never gone camping, but this seems like a great place to enjoy peace, quiet, and the beauty of God's creation. I was told by the bus driver on my first excursion that the brown bears outnumber the people here 4 to 1. I told my friend who traveled with me that we could camp along with the bears and sing 'Kumbaya, My Lord.'

This morning, we went on a smaller boat to whale watch.

What Are You Waiting For?

It's interesting that the birds know best where the whales are. If you follow the birds, you'll usually find the whales. The ways that the whales hunt the fish draw the birds in large numbers. It was fascinating to watch all of the birds swarming around the area where the whales were. One whale came up out of the water several times and made huge splashes. They call this 'breaching.' It was beautiful. They were humpback whales. They're here in abundance.

I had a great time, but I'm still waiting to see the orcas. Orcas and blue whales are what I really want to see. I didn't even know about blue whales until a couple of weeks before this trip. I learned about them by watching a whale documentary. I was amazed at the size of blue whales. They're now on my must-see list. Sometimes, we don't even know what's out there to be seen. I'm so thankful that God continues to open my eyes and my understanding to more and more new things.

Each day, we've been meeting new people at dinner or while standing in line to get on or off the ship. Last night, we met two English women. They're world travelers and have been many places. One had even gone to Antarctica and seen the penguins.

I'm grateful to be here, yet I know there's more. I hear people say that they will never get to come back. One said that she would never be able to buy a fur coat. I don't say those things. I believe that I definitely will be able to come back, but will I want to? There's still so much more to see and do. I believe that there are higher heights to reach for, and reach I will.

It's time to let go. What does letting go look like? What is out of your comfort zone? I'm in Icy Strait Point, Alaska, the second port that the cruise ship has docked in. Before today, I had never been zip lining. When I saw that this was the longest one in the United States, it caught my attention. If I'm going to go zip lining, I may as well do it somewhere where there will be amazing scenery. What better place to zip line than in Alaska? This is definitely out of my comfort zone. Usually, new things are.

I'm not an 'adrenaline junkie.' I'm not a thrill seeker when it comes to roller coaster rides and things like that. However, I knew that if I was going to come all the way to Alaska, I needed to do some new things that were out of my comfort zone. The two things I chose were zip lining and dog sledding. Dog

I Found God Outside of Church

sledding will take place tomorrow in Juneau. I'll ride a helicopter (another first) to Mendenhall Glacier where I'll get to dog sled!

As for the zip lining, my friend traveling with me also zip lined today for the first time. I had a certain amount of anticipation or nervousness, but I think hers was much more intense than mine. This almost calmed me in a way to see how nervous others were and that I wasn't alone in the way that I was feeling.

We got on a bus that would take us to the top where we would get harnessed in. The bus driver told us that it was a 40-minute ride to the top. We thought that maybe he was joking, but no, it really was a 40-minute drive. We were told that the line is approximately 1,300 feet high. This is higher than the Empire State Building in New York. That is high! It's probably good that we didn't have a lot of time once we were up there to think about it.

As we were standing on the platform waiting, the anticipation built. Fear tried to grip me. I literally had to say no to the fear that tried to come. I was telling the others around me that this was going to be great. Of course, I also had to battle the same types of uncomfortable feelings that they were. Most of us were first-time zip liners.

There were six harnesses for six people to go at a time. I was placed in the number 3 slot. I got my action camera, which I had bought specially for this trip, attached to my harness with a large clip. I was hoping that the camera would record for the whole drop, which is about 90 seconds.

As we were waiting for our turn on the platform, I heard in my head the words from an older song called 'I Will Survive.' The zipline company was playing some sort of upbeat music, but none in my group were feeling particularly upbeat. Some were questioning why they had signed up for this. Most of us had no idea just how high this was.

I don't know how others operate, but for this one, they have you sit in the harness, and then, they attach stuff over your chest and between your legs. Meanwhile, you're supposed to hold your legs straight out with your feet up against this steel-looking door. While you're sitting there, you can't see down because of the door. This is probably good; otherwise, they might have some medical emergencies taking place at this

What Are You Waiting For?

point.

All of the sudden, one of the guys working there counts, 'One, two, three,' and then, the doors fling open making a very loud sound. It reminds me of the sound that the doors at a horse race make when they're flung open. It's loud and fast.

Before you know it, you're moving rapidly. It felt like I was plummeting to my death. Without thinking, I closed my eyes as it felt like my stomach had left my body and gone to another planet. Initially, the pressure and speed were very intense.

Within a short time, I realized that I was still alive and had not plummeted to my death. I opened my eyes to see that it was absolutely gorgeous around me. Now, we've slowed down and are gliding across the tree tops in beautiful Alaska with the open seas and beautiful, snow-topped mountains ahead,

My thoughts have shifted from, 'I will survive this,' to 'Oh my, this is amazing and beautiful.' It feels like I'm flying through the trees. They had told us that you can feel free to let go and use your arms to help you move either to the right or to the left. I chose to do this, and it was amazing.

First, I let go with both arms. Then, I decided to turn to each side by only extending one arm at a time in the direction that I wanted to go. There's no way to speed up or slow down; that's automatic. It was completely amazing after I realized that I wasn't dead.

It's difficult to explain how I felt when I got off the zip line. I felt more alive than I've ever felt, and I don't mean that in the sense that I didn't die. It was as though something literally awakened inside of me. I was ready to go again after I got off it. I was on a high that I had never experienced before. This was possibly the most exhilarating moment of my life up to this point.

We can be robbed of so much if we let fear get in the way! Fear is in my opinion the biggest thief. And guess where fear comes from? You probably guessed it: Satan. He specializes in stealing. He uses fear to steal from people and to keep them stuck in life. The Word clearly says, 'God has not given us a spirit of fear, but of power and of love and of a sound mind' (II Timothy 1:7, NKJV). Since the spirit of fear isn't from God and because fear tends to steal, I'm confident that it's from Satan, also known as Lucifer. I'm thankful that I said no to fear and

I Found God Outside of Church

didn't let anyone or anything rob me of this experience.

It's time to say no to fear and to live your life now. If there's something that you want to do, find out the cost, save, make arrangements, and go do it. What are you waiting for? Wherever it is that you've always wanted to go, it's time to stop making excuses. Step out and do it!"

The Alaskan cruise in 2017 was my fifth cruise. I've been on four more since then. Each trip has been special in different ways.

I didn't have the funds sitting in the bank when I booked some of the international trips that I've been on, yet God prompted me to book them in faith. I did so, and by the time that the various payments were due, the funds were there. Money should not be an excuse. Sometimes, we have to first step out in faith.

Here's another clip of what I wrote in Alaska:

"Please don't wait to do the things that you have a burning desire to do. Dog sledding on a glacier in Alaska isn't cheap, but I had a sense when I looked at the excursions that this wasn't something that many get the opportunity to do. I knew that it would be an exhilarating and memorable experience that I would never forget. So, I stepped out of my comfort zone to book it. It's four times the cost of some of the other things that I'm doing in Alaska, yet I'm confident that it will be more than worth the cost.

When I considered booking this trip to Alaska, I sensed God saying, 'Why not now?' As I sit here near the pool, enjoying the peace, calm, and sereneness of this moment in time, I'm glad that I listened. Why not now?

I met a woman when I was back home at the beach recently. She was 55. When I told her that I had booked this trip to Alaska, she said that it's time for her to start living her life. Her reason for not doing things is that she doesn't always have someone to travel with.

When I went to Israel in 2016, I didn't feel led to try to have anyone go with me. God prompted me to book a trip with a tour group, so I did. You could let the agency pair you with a roommate of your same gender, or you could pay extra to have your own room. I opted to have my own room.

God has a way of working things out. On that trip, it was

difficult for me to adjust to the 7-hour time change, so I was glad that when I couldn't sleep at night, I could turn the television on without having to worry about disturbing anyone. Not having someone to travel with should not stop you from living your life. I'm speaking from personal experience on this.

There's no good reason to wait to live your life.

My traveling companion on this Alaska trip is a friend from Memphis, Tennessee, where I lived for many years. We had previously worked together. We both said when we booked the trip that we didn't have to do everything together. This wasn't a trip that most people would take more than once in their lives. We agreed that we should both book and do whatever we're interested in individually, and that's exactly what we've done.

There's only one excursion that we both booked and will do together. We'll have plenty of time together on the ship. I think that we'll have a good mix of not being alone yet getting to do the things that we both want to do."

I find it interesting that there's a true cost to amazing things in life. In fact, there are often things that one has to overcome before they can experience the amazing things in life. First, there's the financial cost. A cruise to Alaska including airfare can be a significant cost. The excursions can also be costly. Then, there's the cost of getting uncomfortable and facing one's fears, whatever they may be. Yet, the blessings of stepping out in faith far outweigh all costs. Why do I continue to step out into the unknown? Because every time I do, I experience amazing things that I wouldn't have been able to experience otherwise.

I've given you a few examples of ways that I haven't waited to live my life, regardless of whether or not I had a travel partner and regardless of whether or not it made sense financially at the time.

What are you waiting for? What is that thing that you've always wanted to do? Why not book it now? It's time to live now. Climb to that higher height.

humpback whale
Icy Strait Point, Alaska - 2017

19
Wrap-Up

How did I go from having a broken heart at the bottom of my closet floor in Tennessee to exhilaration on a zip line more than 1,300 feet high in Alaska? How did I go from being a shy, insecure girl who avoided people to moving to a state where I knew no one? How did I travel overseas to Brazil, face rejection in New York, travel to Israel by myself, and dog sled in Alaska? How did I go from staying in the back of a room to try to avoid being noticed to then choosing to stand before groups of people speaking or even being on a worship team? Jesus – the transforming power of Jesus in my life – is the only answer.

No matter what your childhood was like, no matter what choices you've made, and no matter what you've done, God loves you. He wants to take your life and do something amazing with it. He wants you to learn who He created you to be. You are valuable, and He has an exciting life full of adventures waiting for you. Will you say yes to Him today and begin the most exciting journey you will ever take? If you follow Him, I guarantee you that He will allow you to see things you never even dreamed of. I also guarantee you that you'll find more joy and purpose in your life than you ever knew before. It may not be an easy journey, but it will be worth it.

If you've experienced something traumatic, I have compassion for you. Please know that God was not behind what caused your pain. That was Satan. However, God would love to bring healing into your life if you will let Him.

It angers me to think about how many people have been deceived about God through a bad church experience or through someone claiming to be a Christian that isn't. I used to be one of those that was deceived about God. I really didn't know that He is good. I definitely didn't know that He loved me. Hearing and knowing are two very different things. It's so important to personally get to know Him. Once you're saved, you don't have to rely on a priest or a pastor as a go-between between you and God. You can go directly to God in the name of Jesus. Jesus paid a very high price so that we could have direct access to God. Please take advantage of that access that you freely have to the

I Found God Outside of Church

Creator of the universe. He loves you. He really does love you.

Is there anything stopping you from getting to know God more or taking that next step? Is there something in your past that you blame God for? I once had a coworker ask me why God allows people to molest children. I didn't have a good answer for her when she asked me. The truth is that all of us get to make choices. Many refer to this as free will. We're free to choose how we want to live this life. God doesn't make us choose Him or make us live a good life. God doesn't go around controlling everyone like robots.

As important as it is to know that God is real and is good, it's equally important to know that Satan is real, is loose in the world, and plays a big part in the evil that you see and experience.

One thing I know is that God can take the worst situation and somehow bring something good out of it if you will let Him. You may think that there's no way possible in your situation, but what Satan means for evil, God can use for good. I love the Scripture in Genesis 50:20. Let me explain what's happening in this passage. Joseph's brothers hated him. They were jealous of him and wanted to kill him. At the last minute, they decided to sell him instead.

Joseph went through a lot. He was sold as a slave by his own family. Then, he was falsely accused of rape and put in prison for many years for something that he didn't do. He suffered a lot and for a long time, but eventually, God raised him up. Joseph was freed from prison, given favor, and put in a very high position in the country where he lived. The brothers who hated him later came before him begging for food during a time of famine in their country. Joseph could've killed them or imprisoned them. But Joseph chose to forgive them and said these profound words: "You intended to harm me, but God intended it all for good. He brought me to this position so I could save the lives of many people" (Genesis 50:20, NLT). I'm assuming that it may have taken Joseph some time and a lot of life lessons from God to get to a point where he had that perspective.

In my situation, I now know that Satan definitely wanted to harm not only me, but also Chance and his entire family. Satan is no respecter of persons. He'll take out as many people as he

Wrap-Up

can. Satan wanted me to feel hopeless, worthless, and crushed enough so that I would take my own life. Clearly, that didn't happen, although he did try to give me those kinds of thoughts. Also, he clearly wanted to break apart Chance's family. Guess what? Satan failed at that too. To my knowledge, Chance's family is still together, and two months after I moved to Georgia, Chance became a Christian. So, what the enemy Satan intended for evil, God was able to turn around for good in both of our lives once we each turned to God.

While in Georgia, I've healed, grown, and matured leaps and bounds. I've gotten free in many areas, and I now live my life to a much fuller degree than ever before. I'm not shying away from life; rather, I'm embracing it at ever increasing levels and speeds. I have more joy and fulfillment than ever before. All of this is because I've encountered the love of God, trusted Him, and surrendered to Him more and more. The more I say yes to Him, the stronger I get, and the better my life has gotten.

In the story of Joseph, his brothers represent Satan. Satan intends to harm us and can cause us great pain through people. Yet, God wants to take that situation and bring good out of it. He will heal the wounds if you will allow Him to. Then, as He restores you, He can use you to help others going through something similar. Nothing has to be wasted. God can use the worst of situations and bring good out of them. The worst time of my life turned out to be the best time of my life once I let God into that pain, and He healed me. I grew more through having gone through the pain and then overcoming. There's a strength and power in overcoming.

It's time to overcome your past and your pain. Today is the day! Surrender right where you are! Don't put it off another moment! Your healing is now! Your time is now!

Maybe you already said yes to God some time ago but have strayed away. He's calling you back to Himself now.

Maybe you've been holding back from what you know He's called you to do. There's a knowing that you have deep within that you've pushed aside for too long. It's time to now step out in faith. You'll change your life and many others' lives for the better for eternity.

Don't delay. Today is the day that you can change your life. It begins with saying yes.

I Found God Outside of Church

God loves you, and He will never let you down. He's good and faithful. My dear Brazilian friend Kalleb once said, "When man rejects you, God chooses you." Sometimes, people have rejected me; sometimes, I've felt rejected by the church. Yet, God chooses me. He chooses me to be His daughter. He also chooses me to do significant work for His kingdom that will last for eternity. That's why I choose to write this book and bare parts of my soul to you. Jesus is so worth it.

I want to leave you with an important truth about you. You are a masterpiece, and you have purpose. "For we are God's masterpiece. He has created us anew in Christ Jesus, so we can do the good things he planned for us long ago" (Ephesians 2:10, NLT).

www.ingramcontent.com/pod-product-compliance
Lightning Source LLC
Chambersburg PA
CBHW050259120526
44590CB00016B/2418